A REVOLT OF THE NATIVES OF GOA, 1787

By the same author :

Trade and Finance in Portuguese India. A Study of the Portuguese Country Trade, 1770-1840 (New Delhi, 1994)

Goa : Images and Perceptions. Studies in Goan History (Goa, 1996)

Situating Indo-Portuguese Trade History. A Commercial Resurgence, 1770-1830 (Tellicherry, 2003)

Economics of the Tobacco Monopolies in Goa, 1674-1856 (Goa, 2012)

A REVOLT OF
THE NATIVES OF GOA,
1787

THE FORGOTTEN MARTYRS

CELSA PINTO

A REVOLT OF THE NATIVES OF GOA, 1787

THE FORGOTTEN MARTYRS

© Published by

BROADWAY
PUBLISHING HOUSE

SIGNATURE STORE:

1st Floor, Ashirwad Bldg.,Near Caculo Island, 18th June Road,Panjim-Goa.
Tel: 2420677, 6647037, 6647038, Fax: 6647038
Website: *www.bbcbooks.net* Email:*bbcbooks@rediffmail.com*

CACULO MALL:

Caculo Enclave, St. Inez, Panaji - Goa. Tel: 2233338/9

MARGAO:

Paulinoes Building, Ground Floor, Near Popular High School, Comba, Margao-Goa. Tel: 6489777, (M) 9860030339

CANDOLIM:

Landscape Holiday Unit, Ground Floor, Near Dr. Dukles Hospital & Research Centre, Aguada Fort Road, Candolim-Goa.
Tel: 6519777, (M) 9860030339

DUBAI:

Shop No.19, A1 Wahda Bldg., Opp. Deira City Centre Metro Stn.Port Saeed, Deira, P.O. Box: 211373, Tel: +971 4 2500688, (M) +971 558728529
E-mail: *info@booksindubai.com*

ISBN: 978-93-80837-65-9

Printed by Rama Harmalkar 9326102225

Price ₹ 250/-

PREFACE

On the occasion of the 225th year of the attempted revolt of 1787 in Goa, I place before you this monograph, a tribute and a dedication to those men, whose efforts to liberate Goa from the Portuguese rule ended in their supreme sacrifice at the gallows.

It has baffled me a great deal as to why the episode of 1787 is little or not known to the people of Goa, why it has faded from public memory, why its bi-centennary year, in 1987, went unnoticed, why even in this year the opportunity was not seized by regular contributors to local newspapers to recall and report on it, why the event was not deliberated upon, in the quiet and disciplined atmosphere of academic seminars in academic institutions and circles, and why when other freedom fighters are glorified (and rightly so), there was no public recognition or occasion for commemoration.

It is disappointing to point out, that some writers and historians blindly rely on the only book (as per my knowledge) we have on the said revolt, namely *A Conjuração de 1787 em Goa e Varias Cousas desse tempo* by Joaquim Heliodoro da Cunha Rivara published in 1875, which has distortions and errors. Some demonstrate skepticism, disinterest and subject the episode to ridicule. We need to remember that another rebellion (1789) almost identical in nature, in Goa's counterpart in the Atlantic, in far-off Brazil, was and continues to be treated as a national event.

Tiradentes, one the leaders of this rebellion was beheaded on April, 21, 1792. He is worshipped as a patriot and April 21, the day of his execution is a national holiday. The events of 1789 in Minas Gerais, Brazil, just two years after Goa's revolt of 1787, is firmly implanted in the Brazilian consciousness as a symbol of national pride.

It is not, my purpose to take up the judge's mantle and pass a verdict but to stick to the scholar's role, ethics and attitude. Nonetheless, this lack of historical memory and prejudice is unwarranted. It is a truism that the revolt of 1787 was doomed before it began, but it still deserves to be remembered. The Goans might have in 1787 won the fight for independence in a day or two, but did not do so because of a betrayal. Goa's defining, moments of liberation and glory were perhaps by this act, deferred for about 175 years.

A lot of questions haunted me since 1987. In fact I desired to work on this subject for my doctoral degree which even then was close to my heart. But my guide Professor Teotonio R. de Souza diverted my attention and lured me into the world of Indo-Portuguese economic history and for twenty-five long years, I have been treading the economic path. At this historical juncture, (225th year) I could not refrain and restrain myself. I strongly felt the urge to bring forth this work to challenge the claims of Cunha Rivara and to give the event its due place in history. After all, fifteen natives were officially condemned to death, faced public execution, their bodies were quartered and kept on public display. Ten others faced exile or the galleys, and fourteen had languished for twenty years in jails without penalty. Has there been any such happening in the history of Goa's freedom movement?

This book is a serious attempt to retell the story of the intended revolt of 1787. It is based on original documentation — the proceedings of the *Devassa* (Judicial Inquiry) which is mainly composed of the testemonies of 41 witnesses and the depositions (*Autos*) of 46 accused, who were on trial for about six months. The *Devassa* records run into 567 (including the reverse) folios. I was able to personally trace them in the *Maços da India* (loose documents on India) in *Archivo Histórico Ultramarino* at Lisbon way back in 1991, while working on my doctoral thesis. About twenty years later, I have thoroughly examined them to produce this volume. Though it has a nativist approach, I have maintained the balance, as anything else is no doubt unacceptable for any decent unbiassed historian.

It must be confessed that despite my beaver-like efforts, some questions that troubled me remain unanswered. What happened to Fr. Couto and Fr. Gonsalves? Could it be that both the attempted and aborted revolts in Goa (1787) and Brazil (1789) were planned together in Lisbon or elsewhere in Europe?

I hope this book will tease and incite the academic mind, to raise more questions and undertake more research on a subject that till date is badly understood.

The writing of this book has been a long and emotional journey. Many have been the sources of great help and victims of my frustrations. I am greatly indebted to C.K. Mathew, Yvette Rego, Laurita Sardinha, Uttam Raut Dessai and Goretti Pereira who selflessly stood by me, and wish to record my deep gratitude to them. I also extend my thanks to Antonio Manoel Pereira for material on *Inconfidência Mineira* (1789) and Manoel Lobato for arranging to send from Lisbon the prints of the *Devassa* records. Thanks are also due to Khalil Ahmed for offering to publish this book.

Panjim, Goa CELSA PINTO
December 25, 2012

CONTENTS

LIST OF TABLES

LIST OF APPENDICES

ABBREVIATIONS

AHU	*Arquivo Historico Ultramarino*
HAG	Historical Archives of Goa
MI	*Maços de India*
MR	*Monções do Reino*

GLOSSARY

Academia de Marinha	Naval Academy
Alferes	Second Lieutenant
alpendre	porch
alvará	An order issued by the Viceroy or any other high ranking official valid for one year without royal confirmation
arcebispado	archbishopric
arroba	a quarter of a quintal
Autos de Devassa	trial records/proceedings
bala	bullet
balões	boats; vessels
begarim	labourer
bispado	bishopric
boias	carriers of *machila* (a form of transport in Goa)
Brahmin	An upper caste of priests and scholars
Cabo	a military rank
cachorros	young dogs
cafres	blacks
calões	containers; vessels
Capitaens	Captains
capitannia	captaincy
carioca	a native of Rio de Janeiro, Brazil

casados	Portuguese settlers in Goa who were married to local women
cedula	an official document, letter
cesto	a basket with a cover
chito	a note
claustro	cloister
Cofres de Erario	coffers of the Exchequer
communidade	a village community
correspondente	agent or businessman
degredados	the exiled
derrama	local tax
Devassa	a judicial enquiry / trial
Dezembargados do Paco	Royal Board of Justice and the highest court of appeal
feitoria	trading station or an agency in an Asian port
Furriel	a military rank
gales	galleys
Granadeiros	Grenadiers
Inconfidência Mineira	Conspiracy of Minas Gerais (1789)
interrogatorios	questions directed towards the accused
lugar das forcas	area occupied by the army
mulatos	Luso-Africans
mineiros	natives of Rio de Janeiro; mine-owners; miners
navio	a ship
nau	a large ship
Padroado Real	Crown patronage of the Church
palmares	coconut groves
pardau	a coin of Portuguese India equivalent to 300 *reis*
partilhas	shares
patentes superiores	high posts
portador	messenger

Potencias Asiasticas	Asian powers or rulers
pousada	lodging
praças	squares, fortresses
Propaganda Fide	Congregation of the Faith initiated by the Vatican in 1622
Quartel	barracks
quitanda	greengrocery
Reino	kingdom of Portugal
reinois	Portuguese born in Portugal, belonging to the nobility
Relação	High Court of Justice
reo	accused, prisoner
rupia	coinage of Portugues India approximately more than 600 *reis*
santhome	Goan gold coinage
Sargento	Sargeant
semestre	semester
Senado de Camara	Municipal Council
soldado	soldier
sublevação	a revolt or rebellion
sublevar	to revolt or rebel
Tenente	Lieutenant
testemunha	witness
vargeiro	labourer
Vereador	Municipal alderman
xerafim	silver currency of Portuguese India equivalent to five *tangas* or 300 *reis*

1

INTRODUCTION

Mariano Dias in his research paper entitled "Fr. Caetano Vitorino de Faria", in *Essays in Goan History* edited by T. R. de Souza, pointed out that "More than a century has elapsed since, J. H. da Cunha Rivara's *A Conjuração de 1787 em Goa* was published, and it has remained the only source book, all its deficiencies notwithstanding".[1] Despite bias, disparities and errors, Cunha Rivara's work held sway for more than 135 years. Many have been relying on a work that is explicitly written from a colonial angle and is anti-native. After all, Cunha Rivara was a Portuguese and was part and parcel of the colonial administration. There is nothing in his work that speaks against the Portuguese. It is time to bring this to the attention of the academic world.

First and foremost we can gauge the colonial approach in the above-mentioned work, in a preliminary fashion, with words, phrases and sentences that are transcribed below:-[2]

(1) "heinous and abominable crime of revolt and high treason was hatched in the islands."

(2) "Conspirators incited members of the Legions to revolt."

(3) "To persuade the people they (rebels) had recourse to horrible

lies and coercion, assuring them very confidently that this rebellion was not a sin but the will of God and had the blessings of the Pontiff himself."

(4) "The sentence recorded that they (rebels) boasted of assistance from foreign powers, of having thousands of arms and unlimited funds while in fact they had nothing".

No where in the *Devassa* records is there a reference to the 'Pontiff' and to 'unlimited funds'. These are just few illustrations of distortion traced in his book. It is not an overstatement to observe that Cunha Rivara's attempts at distortion are meant to tarnish the image of Goan patriots who laid down their lives at the gallows and remained in the prisons of Lisbon for long years for the cause of liberation. However such an uncomplimentary stance against the natives of Goa does not hold up to scrutiny.

In his work, Cunha Rivara has also indulged in a disinformation campaign to undermine Fr. Caetano Vitorino de Faria (the father of the celebrated Abbe Faria) based in Lisbon, more of whom, we shall dwell upon in the next chapter. But over here, it is important to record, that Mariano Dias in his above-mentioned research paper, has done justice to place Fr. Faria in proper and right perspectives.[3]

It would never be out of place, to place on record Cunha Rivara's errors, some of which are listed below:-[4]

(1) that the date of revolt was fixed for August 10, 1787. There are several dates mentioned in the records.

(2) that the rebel clerics were never tried. This is untrue. The said priests were subjected to a trial. Their depositions during the *Devassa* prove this, but no penalty was imposed.

(3) that Tenente Inacio Toscano and Tenente Luis Nicolao da Costa advised the strategy of poisoning the bread. None of the depositions collaborate this.

(4) that the conspirators had an alliance with Tipu Sultan to end the Portuguese rule in Goa. There are no detailed plans recorded to substantiate this. In fact much relevant research has been undertaken to disprove this viewpoint of Cunha Rivara. Noteworthy is the work of Ernestina Carreira, entitled "Goa in the Reign of Tipu Sultan. International Politics and the Pinto's Conspiracy".[5] The author has also produced a research essay on the matter. It bears the title "Tipu Sultan's Designs on Goa: Fact or Fiction?"[6]

Cunha Rivara's viewpoints have usually revolved round the *Sentença* imposed on the accused on December 9, 1788. He has accepted lock, stock and barrel all the arguments and conclusions arrived at by the Portuguese authorities in the said *Sentença*. As stated earlier, local historians have relied on Cunha Rivara's version. A telling example is the work of a senior historian George Moraes "Contribution of Cunha Rivara to Indian Historiography".[7]

It is time to turn to fact and not fancy or bias and bring forth a totally different line of argument challenging the colonial stance of Cunha Rivara. There is the need to sketch a more accurate picture of the said event.

There have been studies that have focussed on the happenings of 1787, which have captured the author's attention.[8] But none have examined the *Devassa* records in totality. This book is based on the minute details available in the said records — the denunciations, the statements of the witnesses and the *Autos* of the accused.

The *Devassa* proceedings contain an ocean of ideas and views, charges and counter-charges and above all, they reflect the level of the thought and mind of the people undergoing the trial. If we want to understand the *Devassa*, we need to listen to what the records say.

REFERENCES

1. Mariano Dias, "Fr. Caetano Vitorino de Faria", *Essays in Goan History*, ed. T. R. de Souza, New Delhi, 1989, p.139.

2. They are drawn from the English translation of Cunha Rivara's *A Conjuração de 1787 em Goa e varias cousas desse tempo: Memoria História*, which is entitled *Goa and the Revolt of 1787*, ed. Charles Borges, New Delhi, 1996, pp. 37-42 : *passim*.

3. Dias, *op.cit.*, pp. 139-154.

4. Borges, *op.cit.*: *passim*.

5. Ernestina Carreira, "Goa in the Reign of Tipoo Sultan. International Politics and the Pinto's Conspiracy". A paper presented at the Fifth International Seminar on Indo-Portuguese History, Cochin, Jan. 1989.

6. Celsa Pinto, "Tipu Sultan's Designs on Goa: Fact or Fiction?" in *Goa: Images and Perceptions. Studies in Goan History*, Goa, 1996, pp. 18-28.

7. G. M. Moraes, "Contribution of Cunha Rivara to Indian Historiography", *India: Past and Present*, I, n.2 (1984), pp.75-76.

8. Besides the works of Ernestina Carreira and Mariano Dias cited above, the author has examined the following works:-
Maria de Jesus Martires Lopes, *Goa Setecentista: Tradição e Modernidade, 1750-1800*, Lisbon, 1996; Maria de Jesus Martires Lopes, "A Colonia Goesa em Lisboa e O Idéario da Conspiração dos Pintos (1787)", *Arquipélago*, Série Histórica, Ponta Delgada, Vol. 1-1, 1995; Anita Correia Lima de Almeida, "Goa de 1787 e Rio de Janeiro de 1794: Inconfidência no Imperio" in *Portuguese Studies Review*, vol. IX, no. 112, 2001, pp.47-83; Pratima Kamat, *Farar Far. Local Resistance to Colonial Hegemony in Goa 1510-1912*, Goa, 1999.

2

CAUSES OF THE REBELLION

There were a variety of factors both remote and immediate that sparked off the fervent effort to stage a revolt in Goa.

At Lisbon:

Enlightenment, Education and the Evolution of a Nativist Ideology.

The starting point of the project to overthrow the Portuguese rule in Goa was undoubtedly Lisbon. Since the 1770s, Europe was a complex of new ideas, theories and doctrines. Winds of enlightenment blew over Europe largely due to the spirit of liberty spread by the American War of Independence.[1] In the years leading to the French Revolution of 1789, the ideas of liberty, equality, justice, love for one's country, identity of the people, etc. totally engulfed the people of Europe, including the Goans based at Lisbon. The latter were ideologically gripped with the thought of liberating Goa from the clutches of the Portuguese.[2] They were well-informed and displayed a genuine interest in the happenings in Goa. Some of them expressed the desire to return to India to attend to "the roads for the future happiness of Goa".[3]

Though the ideology of liberty was a vital factor for the episode of 1787 in Goa, so also was education. The Oratorians of Goa played a vital role as agents of change, diffusing liberal ideas and promoting, the cause of higher education. Goans over the years had been going to Europe for further studies. Not only the religious but also laymen went there for intellectual formation. In this context, one must mention Fr. Caetano Vitorino de Faria and his son José Custodio, José Antonio Pinto, Joaquim Antonio Vicente, Fr. José Antonio Gonsalves and Fr. Caetano Francisco de Couto. Goan youth who went to Europe to satisfy their aspirations for learning at Lisbon were impacted by projects of reformism, studied natural history, botany, chemistry, pharmacy, etc.[4]

From a letter of Joaquim Antonio based at Lisbon, addressed to Fr. José Antonio Gonsalves at Goa, we gather that the former had completed a *Curso da Marinha* under the renowned Bruneli.[5] In fact, Joaquim Antonio had distinguished himself in his studies and was recognised as one of the best *finalistas* of the *Academia de Marinha*.[6]

A letter of José Antonio Pinto, also residing at Lisbon to his brother Fr. João Baptista Pinto at Goa, indicates the tremendous importance given to global education by Goans in Europe. He opined, that his nephew at Goa be taught French and be admitted in the *Colegio de Rachol*.[7] His advice implied the necessity to nurture a student's intellectuality, which was the need of the hour.

Italy, a great centre for the diffusion of progressive ideas, was another such haunt for pursuing intellectual and cultural formation. It promoted studies, both religious and non-religious, where evidently the ideology of liberalism was assimilated. The contacts with Italy were not new. The first Goan bishops were consegrated by *Propaganda Fide,* as in the case of Mateus de Castro in 1637. Various Goans underwent intellectual formation at Italy, like Fr. Caetano Vitorino de Faria, his son José Custodio and Fr. José Antonio Gonsalves. In fact there was a close nexus between the Goans in Lisbon and those in Italy, which was politico-ideological in nature and was a cause for *movimento cultural das luzes*.[8]

Colónia Goesa

There emerged in Lisbon a colony of Goans consisting of persons of a certain level of culture and civic responsibility who formed the bedrock for the ideological preparation and basis of the nativist rebellion of 1787 in Goa.[9] As indicated earlier, Joaquim Antonio Vicente, Narcise Vicente (perhaps his brother), José Antonio Pinto (son of Inacio Pinto), Fr. José Custodio de Faria and Fr. Caetano Vitorino de Faria were based in Lisbon in the later part of the eighteenth century. Since they lived together they discussed matters relating to their motherland, Goa and these discussions played their own role in sowing the seeds of a secret plan to expel the Portuguese from India.[10]

The Lisbon Goans in their letters back home demonstrated a deep love for their land. With the winds of change blowing over Portugal, Europe and the rest of the world they had opportunities to dwell on the lot of the Goans in Goa. They were well aware of life both in Goa as well as in Europe.[11] Their reflections indicated their discontentment towards the Portuguese rule. They pointed out to a non-existent progress in Goa and the need for reforms. One issue that was focussed on by José Antonio Pinto in his letter to his brother Fr. João Baptista Pinto, in Goa, was the poor utilisation of cultivable land. He referred to the availability of extensive land in Ponda for the cultivation of café, mandioca and pepper. He referred to Luis José Guinete, an Italian who had accompanied the Archbishop of Craganore back to India, and who had, perhaps, expertise in the matter. Also, very categorically he makes a reference to their brother Tenente Manoel Caetano

Pinto (at Goa) who was denied the *patente* of *Capitão de Infantaria*. He states that the higher and superior military posts went to the *reinois* and persons of little merit even *degredados*. In his opinion only Goans would know the "*caminhos de sua futura felicidade*".[12]

To fulfil these objectives, some of the Lisbon Goans showed their desire to return back to their "*infeliz Patria*" and this led to much activity in Lisbon.[13] They toyed with the idea of the liberation of Goa and therefore offered their usefulness and expertise for the realisation of a project. They worked to prepare relatively viable plans, to be implemented by Fr. José Antonio Gonsalves who emerged as the real and true leader of the attempted rebellion of 1787.

It would be no exaggeration to say that long after Fr. Gonsalves left Lisbon for Goa, he occupied a special place in the lives of the natives of Goa living in Lisbon. Their letters to him are evidence enough.[14] A similar consideration was also extended to Fr. Couto, another *mentor da intentona*".[15]

The letters of the Goans at Lisbon to Goa reflected their contacts with Italy (*encomendas para Livorno*). They also provided news of the happenings in Portugal—death of D.José, the dislocation of the Lisbon court to Figueira, climatic alterations, shortage of provisions, problems of sanitation, etc. There are references to commercial contacts between Goa and Macau, the need to despatch cardamom seeds from India, etc.[16]

At Lisbon, discontentment amongst the Goans was also due to the fact, that little attention was paid to their grievances at the Lisbon court, even by the Queen.

It is in Lisbon, that the seeds of a nativist revolt in Goa were sown. Not only were plans drawn up, but also legislation collected, compiled and prepared for a future government.[17] No sooner Fr. Couto reached Goa in May 1786, a kick start was given to the operations of the project that was hatched in Lisbon.[18]

Role of Fr. Caetano Vitorino de Faria

Fr. Caetano Vitorino de Faria was the oldest of the Goan residents in Lisbon and the patriarch, protector and mainstay of the Indian community in that city. He was a '*figura de referencia*' for the Goan youth in search of education in the Portuguese or even the European universities.

Fr. Faria first arrived in Lisbon in 1771. He studied for his doctorate at Rome from 1772 to 1777 and returned to Lisbon shortly after.[19] He soon gained favourable acceptance there, through the good offices of Fr. João Baptista de S. Caetano, a Benedictine and the Apostolic Nuncio de Tyro. He built up substantial influence and found easy access to the homes of Cardinal da Cunha and several noblemen. Being a man of education, he had deep knowledge of many matters. His court position and the faith that the Queen reposed in him, gave him access to information about the developments in Portugal and abroad.

Under the above circumstances, it was not surprising, that he used his influence in the Lisbon court to serve best the interests of the people of Goa. He was the principal mediating link between Goa and Lisbon. He protested against all *Ordens Regulares* and all ecclesiastical, civil and military authorities, in fact the entire administration of Portuguese India, which he found vexatious and which he felt, indulged in the maltreatment of the natives.[20] For instance, he was critical of the prevailing system of bribery in the selection of army recruits. He submitted to the authorities various plans for reform in Goa, most of which focussed on issues pertaining to the Congregation of the Oratory.[21]

Appreciable, were the efforts of Fr. Faria to end colour discrimination in Goa. It was his staying power and ability to convey and convince, that compelled Martinho de Melo e Castro,

Secretario of the *Estado da India*, in his letter to the Goa Government, dated March 21, 1779 to send instructions that all the religious orders set up in Goa, had to admit native novices and that they were to be treated on equal terms. It may be noted that Indians were denied entry, despite orders prevailing since 1774.[22]

Fr. Faria interceded forcefully with the Crown on behalf of Inacio Pinto of Candolim, to do away with the disparity in the use of the veil by nuns. Native nuns had to use the white veil while their Portuguese counterpart used the black veil. This 'veiled' discrimination was done away with.[23] It was a sign of changing times.

There was the issue of limited admission of the natives of Goa to civil and military posts in their own land. Due to Fr. Faria's intervention, Martinho de Melo e Castro reinforced the earlier orders, by the letter of March 21, 1779 and thereby partially dispelled the growing dissatisfaction.[24]

Likewise by the letter dated January 25, 1783 addressed to the Bishop of Cochin, the latter was instructed to carry out the reform of the two Franciscan provinces of India.[25] This was all due to the concerted efforts of Fr. Faria who played his cards with prudence.

We may sum up with the viewpoint of Mariano Dias, that Fr. Faria should be known and recognised as a patriot, who used his privileged position in the Lisbon court, for the advancement of Goa and the Goans in the last part of the eighteenth century and that he is wrongly remembered as the father of the celebrated and internationally renowned Abbe Faria.[26]

It is commonly believed that the intended rebellion of 1787 was the brainchild of Fr. José Antonio Gonsalves and Fr. Caetano Francisco de Couto. The truth is that the said rebellion was engineered by Fr. Faria as a legitimate reaction to Cariattil's elevation, as the first Indian *Padroado* Archbishop of Craganore.

Fr. Faria was the mastermind behind the plot to displace the Portuguese and to drive them out of Goa, as his hopes to be the first *Padroado* Archbishop, occupying the *Arcebispado* in Se Provincial at Goa were dashed, when this post went to D. Frei Manuel de Santa Catarina by an order issued on November 21, 1784. The hopes of Fr. Gonsalves and Fr. Couto who had been eying the vacant bishoprics of Craganore and Mylapore, met with the same fate. Goan priests were bypassed in favour of South Indian St. Thomas clerics.[27]

At Goa:

The Political Situation

It has to be noted that the Goa Government headed by Governor Francisco da Cunha e Menezes in 1787, was grappling with serious problems. Goa was surrounded by near hostile forces.

There was a temporary lull with the Bhonsles, due to the suspension of hostilities and with the signing of a treaty. However the army was constantly in a state of readiness to handle the foe. There was also the fear of a Tipu Sultan invasion. The Mysorean ruler had conquered all the territories from Kanara and Sunda upto the fort of Piro (Sadashivagad). The presence of Tipu Sultan in the vicinity of Goa spelt danger. The Sunda king who had suffered much loss of face when he was deprived of his kingdom and had to accept Portuguese asylum, was leaving no stone unturned to get back his lost dignity and lands, with the help of the Marathas and other rulers.

The Goa Government faced problems at home as well. Marechal de Campo, Francisco Antonio da Viega Cabral, was undergoing a prison sentence because of his conflicts with the Governor and besides the military *quadros* faced deficiency.[28]

But despite this apparently perilous situation, it goes to the credit of the Portuguese government that it followed a policy of neutrality with the British allied with the Marathas *vis-à-vis* Tipu Sultan, backed by the French. In the intercine rivalry between the said powers, Goa was not only a neutral centre but also an international mediator. With the French, the Portuguese had commercial and diplomatic contacts. Towards Tipu Sultan a policy of reconciliation was followed.[29]

Pombaline Reforms

It is interesting to note that in the last quarter of the eighteenth century, Goa witnessed momentous changes. Reforms initiated by the celebrated Marques de Pombal were largely responsible for creating an atmosphere of revolt.

By the *Alvará Régio* of June 28, 1759 D. José abolished Jesuit education that prevailed for almost two hundred years. A *Republica de Letras* was set up. The Pombaline reform of Humanities included Latin, Greek, Rhetoric and Poetry, Rationalism and Morality. By the *Carta de Lei* of November 6, 1772, 358 posts of *Professores* of Latin, Greek, Rhetoric, Philosophy, Rationalism and Morality and 479 posts of *Mestre de Ler, Escrever e Contar* were created. This had a tremendous impact on Portugal and its colonies. It led to the formation of an *elite letrada ultramarina*.[30]

We have evidence to emphasize that the Pombaline regime was responsible not only for initiating a crusade against ignorance and fanaticism, hypocrisy and superstition but also for focussing on a network of basic education with the passing of *Aulas Regias*. In Goa, however, the latter made little impact and became extinct by 1792, due to lack of students.[31]

Apart from all this, of significance was the Decree of April 2, 1761 a Pombaline legislation, re-affirmed in 1774. In a significant departure from established norms, it removed the barriers that divided the *reinois* and the natives in Goan society. Despite the rights bestowed by this reform on the natives, there was still resistance to them from religious orders. In 1779 the Provincial of the Franciscans refused to admit natives in their order and in 1786 this act was repeated.[32] Such rank discrimination festered and fomented resentment leading to the revolt.

The majority of the rebels belonged to the Brahmin caste, which enjoyed an elevated place in the social hierarchy of Goa. It was this group that welcomed, adopted and assimilated the projects of the Pombaline era: Men of letters, priests, professors etc. were integrated in the Indo-Portuguese society. They had moved to Portugal to get a good intellectual formation and longed for independence.[33]

The reign of D. José was thus a turning point, which brought about notable transformations. It was a landmark in the history of Portugal. However D. Maria I who succeeded him, turned the clock back.

Colour Bar

Our attention shall now be centred on a distinct policy of colour discrimination embedded in the Portuguese colonial system for centuries. Though the Pombaline era changed this, preferences and differences continued to exist. Sharp fissures continued to prevail in Goan society. It was the local clergy who were the first to resent and react to this discrimination. [34] The discontentment in this group grew more pronounced with time, because during the Pombaline administration they had enjoyed some measure of equality.

The same could be said of the military. The natives were never conceded *patentes superiores*, which seriously hindered their professional growth, specially when the policy of the Lisbon government was for recruiting local staff.[35]

In 1781 in the *Camara Geral de Bardez*, the natives were not allowed to occupy *conezias* and preference was shown for *reinois*. This was a clear case of racial segregation.[36]

Social Developments

Goa, in the second half of the eighteenth century, was in a state of flux. But one saw in it some interesting social developments. For instance, the number of Portuguese deserters who moved to Bombay and the neighbouring states was considerable. In 1757 more than 500 of them went to Bombay, Vengurla, etc.[37] The help needed by the Goa authorities was thereby reduced and this was to the advantage of the rebels.

The Viceroy of Goa, Conde de Ega had observed the reluctance of the natives to participate in the Portuguese military service.[38] To iron out this problem, a ban on pain of harsh punishment, was imposed on the use of the expression '*negro*' or '*cachorro*'. It had become clear to Conde de Ega, that white superiority was largely responsible for the indifference shown by the natives to Portuguese interests.[39]

Another interesting phenomenon was the declining strength of the regular European clergy. This re-defined the position and the relevance of the regular clergy recruited from amongst the natives. The policy of recruiting priests of native origin had certain consequences. Not only because of their abundant number but also because of the creation of a group of natives who would be good for religion, but also good for civil and political matters.[40]

Goan priests rose steadily in pre-eminence up the ladder of the ecclesiastical hierarchy and began to exercise their privileges and prerogatives. They had the support of *Propaganda Fide*. The first Goan bishops were ordained by this body—Mateus de Castro in 1637.[41]

The Pombaline reforms had established the equality of the natives and the *reinois*. This created conditions for the rise of the natives of the Brahmin caste. Members of this caste were able to vastly improve their standing. They were not only priests but many of them occupied public posts. They even functioned as ambassadors and envoys in neighbouring kingdoms.[42] This explains why the principal persons behind the plot to overthrow the Portuguese rule in 1787 were mainly of Brahmin origin.

This period socially elevated the *luso-descendentes* and saw their rise and emerging influence due to the Pombaline reforms. Earlier they were deprived of this privileged position and enjoyed little social prestige.[43] Their elevation held them in good stead in the next century.

Conspiracy of 1786 in Calcutta

A conspiracy of the English in Calcutta was found out in 1786. The latter vigorously opposed the parliamentary effort to establish rigorous control over the private assets of the officials of the English East India Company. In all probability Fr. Caetano Vitorino de Faria, who had privy to news at the Lisbon court, had known this fact.[44] This might have impacted some natives of Goa to stage a rebellion against the Portuguese.

Immediate Cause

To top all this, the final straw on the camel's back was the confirmation of Fr. Jose Cariattil as Archbishop of Craganore, the appointment of D. Frei Manuel de Santa Catarina, a Portuguese as the Archbishop of Goa in November 1784 and the appointment of two priests from the Syro-Malabar rite as bishops. These developments deeply hurt the feelings of Fr. Faria, Fr. Gonsalves and Fr. Couto as they went against their interests.

As a consequence of the cummulative factors described above, the history of Goa is landmarked by a serious attempt in 1787 to end the Portuguese regime in the *Estado da India*.

REFERENCES

1. One of the leaders of the intended revolt, Fr. Caetano Francisco de Couto had clandestinely brought to Goa from Portugal, a book *Nova America Ingleza.*

   Source: AHU: *MI* Maço 155 (153), Devassa, Auto No. 11, Statement of Fr. Caetano Francisco de Couto.
2. AHU: *MI* Maço 155 (153), Devassa, Auto No.2, Statement of José Luis Guinete; doc. dted. 20 Sept. 1786.
3. Maria de Jesus dos Martires Lopes, "A Colónia Goesa em Lisboa e o Idéario da Conspiração dos Pintos (1787)" *Arquipélago*, Série Histórica, Ponta Delgada, vol. I-1, 1995, p. 248.
4. Anita Correia Lima de Almeida, "Goa de 1787 e Rio de Janeiro de 1794: Inconfidência no Imperio" in *Portuguese Studies Review*, vol. IX, no. 112, 2001, pp.47-83;
5. AHU: *MI* Maço 155 (153), doc. dtd. 20 Sept. 1787.
6. Martires Lopes, *op.cit.*, p. 250.
7. AHU: *MI* Maço 155 (153), doc. dtd. 15 March 1787.
8. Martires Lopes, *op. cit.* p. 251.
9. *Ibid.* p. 247.
10. *Ibid.*, pp. 247-248.
11. AHU: *MI* Maço 155 (153), doc. dtd. 15 March 1787.
12. AHU: *MI* Maço 155 (153), doc. dtd. 15 March 1787.
13. AHU: *MI* Maço 155 (153), doc. dtd. 20 Sept. 1787.
14. AHU: *MI* Maço 155 (153), docs. dtd. 20 March 1787; 20 Sept. 1787.
15. Martires Lopes, *op.cit.*, p. 249.
16. *Ibid.*, pp. 250-251.
17. AHU: *MI* Maço 155 (153), doc. dtd. 18 Aug. 1787.
18. AHU: *MI* Maço 155 (153), doc. dtd. 18 Aug. 1787.
19. Mariano Dias, "Fr. Caetano Vitorino de Faria", in *Essays in Goan History*, ed. T. R. de Souza, New Delhi, 1989, p. 145.
20. HAG: *MR* 159B, fl. 499.
21. HAG: *MR* 159B, fls. 499-503v.
22. HAG: *MR* 159B, fl. 592.
23. HAG: *MR* 159B, fl. 558.
24. HAG: *MR* 159B, fl. 525v.
25. Dias, *op. cit.*, p. 144.
26. *Ibid.*, p.145.
27. Charles J. Borges, ed., *Goa and the Revolt of 1787*, New Delhi, 1996, p. 13.
28. Maria de Jesus Martires Lopes, *Goa Setecentista Tradição e Modernidade*, Lisboa, 1996, p. 298.
29. *Ibid.*, pp. 298-299.
30. Almedia, *op.cit.*, pp. 47-83:*passim*

31. *Loc. cit.*
32. *Loc. cit.*
33. *Loc. cit.*
34. Borges, *op.cit.*, p.12.
35. Martires Lopes, *Goa Setecentista, op.cit.*, p. 300.
36. *Loc.cit.*
37. *Ibid.*, p. 301.
38. *Loc.cit.*
39. *Borges*, *op.cit.*, pp.14-15.
40. Martires Lopes, *op.cit.*, p.302.
41. *Loc. cit.*
42. *Loc. cit.*
43. *Loc. cit.*
44. *Ibid.*, p. 306.

3

THE REBELS

Hatching the Plot

The plot to end the Portuguese domination in Goa had been effectively conceived and born in Lisbon. It was a matter of necessity rather than opportunism. Deeply entrenched in it and zealously committed to it were Fr. Caetano Vitorino de Faria, José Antonio Pinto, Joaquim Antonio Vicente, Fr. José Antonio Gonsalves and others. In fact, the idea to stage a rebellion against the whites in Goa at the earliest, was pioneered by Fr. Faria.

Upon journeying back to Goa from Lisbon, on board the ship *Santissimo Sacramento e Senhor do Bom Fim*,Fr. Gonsalves had in his company Fr. Caetano Francisco de Couto. After passing by the Cape of Good Hope and when they were on easier terms, Fr. Gonsalves disclosed to Fr. Couto the said plot and the plan of action. Together they set up for themsleves the challenging task of working for its execution, with a deep sense of urgency. It was not going to be smooth and uncontested.

Fr. Gonsalves disembarked in South India, with the obvious intention of garnering help there. He took a detour to visit Travancore, Cochin and Tellicherry, on the look out for manpower and finance needed to execute the said plans. On the otherhand,

Fr. Couto headed for Goa, reached this port in May 1786 and began work in earnest to prepare and build up the courage and morale of some natives to join the movement for over-throwing the Portuguese regime. He targeted his friends, relatives and fellow clerics.

Towards the end of 1786 or perhaps in January 1787, Fr. Gonsalves arrived at Goa. Several persons, who were by and large spirited and strong-willed were ready to take up the challenge.[1] Perhaps the first meeting, relating to the plot, was held at the residence of the Pintos of Candolim. Apart from Fr. Gonsalves and Fr. Couto, Fr. João Baptista Pinto and Tenente Manoel Caetano Pinto of the Legion of Ponda (both of them were sons of Inacio Pinto of Candolim) were present.[2]

The Ringleaders [3]

Fr. Gonsalves and Fr. Couto were doubtlessly the ringleaders of the plot to execute the intended revolt. But Fr. Gonsalves can easily be identified as the chief planner and organiser of the said rebellion. This viewpoint is well-supported by the records.

Fr. Gonsalves was a native of the parish of *Nossa Senhora de Piedade* on the island of Divar. He was a well-educated cleric. His upbringing and formation at the *Seminario de Chorão* was with distinction and he was ordained priest in 1772 when twenty-five years of age. In 1780, he was Professor of Philosophy in the said seminary. In 1781, he renounced this post and left for Lisbon on his way to Rome, to acquire a doctorate from *Propaganda Fide*. As he was supported by the *Congregação de Propaganda Fide*, we see that he adopted a hostile attitude towards the *Padroado Português do Oriente*. He was very much a realist. His brother was also a priest and Professor of Latin Grammar.

Fr. Caetano Francisco de Couto was a native of Panjim who studied Theology at the *Seminario de Chorão* and was considered as a serious student. He was in Cochin for three years handling the administration of the *bispado* (bishopric). On being involved in a series of disputes with the Franciscans of the Malabar, he was relieved of his post. He then left for Lisbon in the monsoon of 1780 or perhaps 1781 to plead his case before the Crown.

The Pinto Link

The revolt of 1787 in Goa is commonly called the Pintos' Revolt (*Sublevação dos Pintos*), yet strangely, the *Devassa* records and other official documentation do not make any reference of this kind. The Pinto family alone and in its entirety did not hatch the plot and plan the execution of the said rebellion. The proposed revolt was not exclusively the handiwork of the Pintos. Yet none can deny their deep involvement as indicated by the records.

José Antonio Pinto, the son of Inacio Pinto, a well-known name in influential circles, was under the tutelage of his relative Fr. Caetano Vitorino de Faria and linked with the birth of the proposed revolt in Lisbon. Besides, his two brothers Fr. João Baptista Pinto and Tenente Manoel Caetano Pinto, together with other relatives like his brother-in-law Manoel Pinto of Saligão, played an active role in the planning and execution of the proposed rebellion in Goa.[4]

The Pintos were a prominent and influential family of Candolim. Inacio Pinto and his elder brother Antonio João Pinto enjoyed the additional distinction of both being recipients of coats -of- arms from the Portuguese Government in 1771.[5] The ancestral home of the Pintos at Candolim was a showpiece in Bardez built in the middle of the seventeenth century by an Italian Catalini.[6] It was in this palatial mansion that the first meeting of the rebels was held. The sons of Inacio Pinto namely Fr. João Baptista Pinto and Tenente Manoel Caetano Pinto were present at this meeting. It is said that the revolt owes its name to the conspiracy meetings that were held in this mansion.[7] Interestingly the conspiracy plans as reflected in the trial records disclose that Inacio Pinto had been selected by the rebels to head the proposed future independent Republic in Goa.[8]

In fact much before August 1787, the Pintos worked in the interest of the natives of Goa including themselves. Inacio Pinto had submitted a petition to the Queen through Fr. Caetano Vitorino de Faria, praying for a decree allowing his daughters and grand daughters and those of his brother Antonio João Pinto, to become nuns of the black veil of Santa Monica at Goa, with the same dowry and honours as those of the Europeans. He requested that this facility be also extended to all other lay nuns.[9] Although the former wife (a nun) of the said Fr. Caetano Vitorino de Faria was the first to enjoy this honour, in 1779, an order was issued by the Lisbon court extending this privilege to all.

It needs to be noted that a letter dated October 1787 addressed to Martinho de Castro e Melo, written by Dezembargador Sebastião José Ferreira Barroco, who was associated with the trial proceedings, pointed out that the Pintos of Candolim were known to be very proud (*mais soberbos*) and very opposed (*mais oppostos*) to everything that was Portuguese.[10]

The Pintos did pay a heavy price for their involvement. While Inacio Pinto was spared arrest perhaps because of his advanced age and his son José Antonio Pinto at Lisbon escaped arrest, his two other sons faced harsh punishments. Fr. João Baptista Pinto languished in jails of Goa and Lisbon for about twenty years and Tenente Manoel Caetano Pinto faced public execution and was a martyr to the cause.[11]

Composition of the Rebels.

Fr. Gonsalves and Fr. Couto were able to rally round themselves, through dint of hard work and charisma, a comprehensive mixture of both secular and non-secular persons mainly of Brahmin origin. Along with these priests one should not forget the role of Fr. Caetano da Silva, Vicar of S. Lourenço de Linhares. Appendix 3.1 enlists those rebels and suspects who underwent trial.

A large number of the rebels were parish priests who commanded a position of influence with their parishioners. They were supported by relatives and friends. Table 3.1 drawn from the trial records gives us a concrete picture.

Some of the rebels were members of the military, particularly of the Legions of Ponda and Bardez—four *tenentes*, some *sargentos*, *cabos* and *soldados*, a *cirurgião mor* and his assistant. Those who supported the plans to stage a revolt against the Portuguese also included businessmen like Sebastião de Noronha and João de Souza Onorcar, *vargeiros*, *begarins* and even students.[12] Susprisingly an Italian from Milan was on several occasions seen in the company of Fr. Gonsalves. He attended meetings and assemblies held at Pilerne, Pomburpa and other places. Undoubtedly he was an accomplice. He knew to produce paper, glass and stamps, to cultivate and produce wines and had knowledge of astrology and the elements of Euclid.[13] But when questioned by Rafael Marcos at Pilerne about his profession he stated that he was busy learning about God.[14] The authorities suspected that his services would be used to stage the revolt and also for the future government.

Table 3.1
RELATIVES / RELATIONS OF THE REBELS

Sr. No.	Rebel / Suspected Rebel / Witness	Relation/Relative (whether Rebel / Suspected Rebel/Witness)	Nature of Relationship
1.	Fr. José Antonio Gonsalves	Fr.Luis Antonio Gonsalves	Brother
		Manoel Francisco Gonsalves	Brother
2.	Fr. Caetano Francisco de Couto	Fr. Diego Caetano de Couto	Brother
		Manoel Luis	Brother-in-law
		Fr. Luis Caetano de Souza	Relative
		Fr. Inacio Xavier Monis	Relative
		Caetano de Couto	Relative
3.	Fr. Miguel Alvares	Fr. Vicente Alvares	Brother
		Fr. João Alvares de Souza	Brother
		Manoel Francisco Gonsalves	Brother-in-law
		Geraldo Ferreira	Relative
4.	Fr. João Baptista Pinto	José Antonio Pinto	Brother
		Tenente Manoel Caetano Pinto	Brother
		Manoel Pinto	Brother-in-law
		Fr. Caetano Vitorino de Faria	Relative
5.	Tenente Nocolao Luis Costa	Salvador (Alvares) da Costa	Brother
6.	Tenente Pedro Luis Gonzaga	Inacio Caetano Lopes	Relative
7.	Marcelino de Noronha	David F. Viegas	Relative

Source: AHU: *MI* Maço 155 (153), Devassa: *passim*.

Geographically, the rebels were chiefly from the provinces of Ilhas, Bardez and Salcette (Table 3.2). But there were a few from the New Conquest areas, mainly Ponda.

Table 3.2

NATIVE PLACE / PLACE OF RESIDENCE OF THE REBELS / SUSPECTS

Province	Native Place *	Place of Residence
Ilhas	17	20
Bardez	16	15
Salcette	9	2
Ponda	1	9

Source: AHU: *MI* Maço 155 (153), Devassa: *passim*

* One of the rebels was from Milan, Italy and another was from Onor, South India.

Relating to the place of origin of the rebels (and suspects as obtained from the records), most of them (seventeen) were from Ilhas — Piedade, Panjim, Chorão, Mandur, Santa Cruz, Taleigão etc.—, sixteen from Bardez mainly Candolim, Pilerne, Pomburpa, and Aldona, nine from Salcette i.e. from Assolna, Nagoa-Verna and Chicalim and one from Ponda. Narba Naique was the native and Sardessai of Ponda.

Relating to the place of residence, twenty of the rebels were residents of Ilhas (Piedade, Panjim, Chorão etc.), fifteen of Bardez (Pilerne, Candolim, Saligão, Anjuna, Pomburpa, Moira etc.) two of Salcette and nine lived in Ponda, most of them in the military quarters at the Legion of Ponda.

Most of the rebels and their accomplices were in the age group fo 30 to 49 years i.e. about seventeen in the age group of 30 to 39 and sixteen in the age group of 40 to 49. (Table 3.3) This indicated that most of rebels were in the prime of their life. Very few i.e. about four of them were in their fifties. and one was sixty years of age. The oldest was Manoel Luis of Candolim who was about seventy years of age.

Table 3.3

THE AGE OF THE REBELS / SUSPECTED REBELS

Age group (in years)	No. of Persons
20-29	5
30-39	17
40-49	16
50-59	4
60-69	1
70-79	1

Source: AHU: *MI* Maço 155 (153) Devassa: *passim*.

From Table 3.4 we gather that seventeen clerics and twenty-nine secular or non-religious, underwent trial and were implicated in the intended revolt, clearing a grave misconception that the revolt of 1787 was strictly of the clergy. Of the twenty-nine non-religious persons, thirteen belonged to the army—Legions of Ponda and Bardez bearing the ranks of *Capitão*, *Tenente*, *Sargento*, *Cabo* and *Soldado*, four were businessmen, two were landlords (owners of farms), and nine were either in service or belonged to the labour class.

From the *Devassa* records it is evident that out of the 46 persons charged and tried, all except one belonged to the Christian community. Narba Naique, a Hindu, who held the position of *Cabo* of one of the *Partidos,* was submitted to judicial inquiry. He was however acquitted. Besides, as indicated earlier, the only non-native to be party to the said rebellion was José Luis Guinete, Italian by origin.

Table 3.4

THE OCCUPATION / PROFESSION OF THE REBELS / SUSPECTED REBELS

Clergy			Military								Others				
Parish Priests	Others	Total	Capitão	Tenentes	Sargentos	Cabos	Soldados	Cirurgião-mor	Ajudante de Cirurgia	Total	In Service/ Labour Class	Business-men	Land-lords	No longer a Soldado	Total
6	11	17	1	4	1	4	1	1	1	13	9	4	2	1	16

Source: AHU: *MI* Maço 155 (153), Devassa: *passim*

REFERENCES

1. AHU: *MI* Maço 155 (153), doc. dtd. 15 Dec. 1787.
2. AHU: *MI* Maço 155 (153), doc. dtd. 26 Sept. 1787.
3. Fr. Couto confessed that Fr. Gonsalves and himself were the leaders of the attempted rebellion, that they had planned to liberate the natives of Goa from the Portuguese rule so that they would become the rulers of the land.

   Source: AHU: *MI* Maço 155 (153), Devassa, Auto No.11, Statement of Fr. Caetano Francisco Couto.
4. AHU: *MI* Maço 155 (153), Devassa, Auto No. 18, Statement of Fr. Luis Caetano de Souza.
5. The author is a direct descendant of Antonio João Pinto.
6. Pratima Kamat, *Farar Far*, p. 157.
7. *Ibid.*, p. 108.
8. AHU: *MI* Maço 155 (153) Devassa, *Testemunha Referida*, Statement of Fr. Felipe de Melo.
9. HAG: *MR* 159B, fl. 558.
10. AHU: *MI* Maço 155 (153), doc. dtd. October 1787.
11. Whether they faced the heat or were left in the cold, this misfortune did not kill the rebellious spirit of the Pintos of Candolim. Prof. T. R. de Souza has pointed out that they were involved in local rebellions on the borders of British territories in 1844.

    Source: Charles J. Borges, *Goa and the Revolt of 1787*, 1996, p.14.
12. AHU: *MI* Maço 155 (153), Devassa: *passim.*
13. AHU: *MI* Maço 155 (153), Devassa, Auto No. 2, Statement of José Luis Guinete; Auto No. 8, Statement of Fr. Miguel Alvares.
14. AHU: *MI* Maço 155 (153), Devassa, Witness No. 33, Statement of Rafael Marcos.

4

PLOTTING AND PLANNING: THE *ASSEMBLEAS*

As indicated earlier, Fr. Gonsalves and Fr. Couto spearheaded the movement for a revolt, that was daring, and relentlessly worked for it. Several persons both religious and secular joined it. Enormous care was taken to draw up strategies, in a bid to stage the revolt successfully.

On the basis of the evidence available in the *Devassa* records, it is clear that the *modus operandi* included the holding of *assembleas* and meetings clustered around Parochial Houses attached to churches and residences of rebels. Here Fr. Gonsalves along with others in a sustained manner, engaged in discussions (*praticas*). With some amount of rhetoric he would highlight the ills in the Portuguese administration, specially their vexatious and coercive policies towards the natives of Goa and thereby whip up emotions.

The rebels also indulged in personal and one-to-one meetings to garner support, for their scheme, hinged on a suitable supply of armed manpower and finance, and everything else needed to make the rebellion a reality and a success. The rebels tried to play their cards with prudence. We have enough evidence to testify this.

Before we examine in detail the various assemblies and individual meetings, held from time to time, for more than seven months, it would not be wrong to highlight the role and the manner in which Fr. Gonsalves conducted himself in the said conferences and meetings, and the issues he focussed upon.

It must be emphasized that Fr. Gonsalves usually occupied a place of predominance and the centrestage at the said assemblies. He was the most articulate and resolute of the rebels. This enabled him to prevail over those assembled. He spoke with a great deal of rancour. Enflamed with anger and hatred towards the Portuguese, his speeches were full of complaints and lamentations that the Lisbon authorities governed as per their whims and fancies, and that they pursued interests contrary to those of their subjects.[1] According to him, the local administration did not care for the natives and held them in poor esteem. He severely criticized the civil and ecclesiastical authorities for their coercive regulations. His targets were the Governor General and the Archbishop of Goa. He stressed that the latter wrote to the Lisbon Government against the local clergy and that the civil government of Dom Federico Guilherme de Souza was guilty of projecting the natives of Goa in poor light. Lisbon authorities were told that the natives were harmful and inefficient.Quoting from a letter that he received about Fr. Caetano Vitorino de Faria, he narrated about the manner in which the Secretario de Estado da India, Martinho de Melo e Castro, behaved towards the said Fr. Faria, that he was insolent, which compelled the latter to use strong language and even threaten a revolt of the natives of Goa.[2]

This was a strategy adopted by Fr. Gonsalves to appeal to the emotions and better sense of the people, to win as many supporters as possible to the cause of the proposed rebellion.

Fr. Gonsalves spoke of Portugal's treatment towards the natives, that there was a definite bias towards them. They were not employed in high-ranking posts. He placed much emphasis on the denial of promotions, awards and honours to them, that they never reached the posts of *Capitaens* and were not given bishoprics.[3] He further said that those who presently occupied high posts were gradually being relieved of them. The authorities planned to remove the *Cabos* in the villages.[4] He deftly played the colour bar card.

Fr. Gonsalves spoke of divine inspiration and sanction in these terms. "God wished to liberate Goa. Let us throw out the Portuguese for us to govern".[5] He expounded and advocated that the future could belong to the natives, that a new government could be established. All were asked to speak to their friends, relatives and even the *casados* about the intended revolt. He said that the natives would be the rulers of the land and live in peace and harmony. They would enjoy honours, grandeur, pre-eminences, posts, etc.[6] They would be promotions such as from *Soldados* to *Cabos*, from *Cabos* to *Sargentos*, from *Sargentos* to *Alferes* and from there the upward climb to the ranks of *Tenentes*, *Capitaens* and *Coroneis*. For this purpose six more legions would be created. He spoke of the establishment of a Republic for which he had brought legislation from Europe.[7] Fr. Gonsalves advanced several new ideas that would help to draw out the natives from their state of oppression and suppression. He pointed out that the natives had suffered enough and should raise the banner of revolt. The speeches of Fr. Gonsalves were characterized by blunt outspokeness.

Fr. Gonsalves also spoke in a manner that many would consider strange and would even doubt the same. Perhaps it was a strategy he used to lure people to join the movement against the Portuguese. For instance he said that the *Estado da India* belonged to the Greek Church. (*Igreja Grega*) under which priests could marry.[8] He also stated that he had brought from Rome, Apostolic letters giving divine sanction to the proposed revolt and that a message had been brought by a priest who came from Rome, stating that it was not a sin to plot and revolt against the Portuguese.[9] Most strange of all was that he stated that he was a favourite in Heaven as he had obtained sanctity for having celebrated mass at the Altar of Our Lady at Rome. He claimed to have revelations and powers to persuade and foment the proposed rebellion as he enjoyed the pleasure of God.[10] He also revealed that Fr. Caetano Vitorino de Faria, at the time of the execution of the rebellion, would move to Rome and provide them all the help that was necessary.[11]

Coming to the *assembleas* and meetings, they began in a concrete manner since January 1787, soon after Fr. Gonsalves returned to Goa from South India. They were organised at Candolim, Panjim, Piedade, Pilerne, Socorro, Anjuna, Penha de França, Pomburpa, Moira, Tivim and other places. In the case of the first three villages / towns they were held at the residences of the Pintos, Fr. Couto and Fr. Gonsalves respectively. But with respect to almost all the others they were held at the Parochial Houses attached to the churches. On most occasions, the rebels would meet before or for the parish feast and remain back as guests. We have the examples of the Feast of San Antonio at Socorro, Feast of Candeus at Pompurpa, and the Feast of Nossa Senhora do Carmo at Moira. Usually the Vicars of the Province of Bardez were invited to the said *assembleas*.[12] Invitations were also extended to some officers and soldiers of the Legions of Bardez and Ponda, so that they could later incite and influence the soldiers in their respective Legions. Others, who could arrange men and money, would also be called. Those who would help to implement the intended revolt were assured of high-ranking posts as per their merit and conduct.[13] Appendix 4.1 gives a tabular picture of the meetings and *assembleas* that were carried out in 1787 in Goa.

Candolim

Sometime before Lent, Fr. Couto accompanied by Fr. Gonsalves, proceeded to the village of Candolim and a conference was conducted in the house of the Pintos, with Fr. João Baptista Pinto and Tenente Manoel Caetano Pinto.[14] Details of the discussions held are not available nor the date of the meeting. But undoubtedly they spoke about the revolt to be staged and this was the start of the planning of the strategies to be adopted. There is little reason not to accept that this *assemblea* marked the beginning for many other *assembleas* that were to follow.

Socorro

This brings us to one of the most important *assembleas*, which was held at Socorro in Serula. On the occasion of the Feast of S. Antonio in early June, Fr. Gonsalves, Fr. Couto, Fr. João Baptista Pinto and others converged at the Parochial House of the church of Socorro and were guests there for 7 to 8 days. The rebels spoke about the proposed rebellion and invited those present to join the movement, which would be in their own interest. At first the Vicar of the church of Socorro was worried and showed reluctance. Eventually, despite misgivings, perhaps he accepted the proposal.[15]

During the trial, Fr. João Baptista Pinto admitted to having stayed in Socorro for about a week as it was raining heavily.[16] But flatly denied that there was any discussion on a revolt.

The reality was that a *pratica* was held at Socorro wherein the ringleaders stated that a revolt was planned so that the natives would become the rulers of the *Estado*. They planned to overpower the Archbishop, the Arsenal and the Governor General with the help of some blacks (*cafres*). They would form a government on the lines of those of Venice. There would be a Republic headed by Inacio Pinto of Candolim.[17]

The rebels stressed the need to end the Portuguese rule in Goa, as it was oppressive, and as it looked down upon the natives and denied them high-ranking posts. For instance, the local clergy were not made bishops. The rebels promised rewarding solutions, that 13 to 14 posts of bishops would be created. They announced that to assist them they had the support of some army officers. Divine sanction was also accorded to the movement.

From the *Devassa* proceedings, we gather that Fr. Diego Benedicto Lobo, who was present at the *assemblea*, noticed that the rebel priests would speak to the Vicar of Socorro privately and in secrecy. Besides Fr. Pedro Caetano José Lobo, Vicar of Tivim in his statement during the trial, indicated that he was told that Fr. Gonsalves tried to instigate those assembled to form a militia company of which he would be the *Capitão*, that Fr. Gonsalves proposed a toast but did not declare the reason for it.[18]

There were several witnesses to the happenings at Socorro. But of vital significance were those who were neighbours—Domingos Pinto and his brother. The former had visited the Parochial House while the *assemblea* was going on and had witnessed the presence of the rebels.[19]

Piedade

In July there was an assembly conducted in the home of Fr. Gonsalves at Piedade, much to the dislike of his brother Fr. Luis Antonio Gonsalves. According to the latter's statement, he objected to the presence of strangers in the *Caza da Conversacão*.[20] This explains why no other meeting was held here, though Fr. Gonsalves was the chief planner and organizer of the attempted revolt.

At the above-mentioned conference were Fr. Gonsalves, his brother Fr. Luis Antonio Gonsalves, Fr. Couto, Fr. Caetano da Silva, Sebastião de Noronha and Tenente Pedro Luis Gonzaga of the Legion of Ponda. They discussed plans for the future revolt. Fr. Gonsalves stated that for its success, men and money were essential and therefore called upon Sebastião de Noronha to help with 400 *rupias* or some men. Noronha stated that he could arrange men but only in the month of September. Tenente Gonzaga promised to do whatever he could to influence the Legion of Ponda for the goals planned by the rebels. It was discussed here that there was the need to contact Narba Naique and Rogu Saunto to join the movement and serve with their *Partidos de Sipais*.[21]

Panjim

The residence of Fr. Couto in Panjim was a haunt for several meetings and *assembleas* much before the return of Fr. Gonsalves. But the momentum changed with the latter's arrival. The two of them took enormous pains to gain loyalty to their cause, through social intervention and other dealings.

Amongst the gatherings held at Panjim, of significance was the one held in the month of May on the occasion of the Feast of Ascension. Present there were not only Fr. Couto and Fr. Gonsalves, but also Fr. Diego Caetano de Couto, brother of Fr. Couto, Salvador da Costa, Fr. Luis Caetano de Souza and Fr. Inacio Xavier Monis. The latter was informed by Fr. Gonsalves of the plan to stage a revolt to end the Portuguese rule in Goa. He requested Fr. Monis to join the movement and gather the support of other people promising them a bright future. But Fr. Monis appeared difficult to convince. A few days later Fr. Gonsalves sent a message (*recado*) through Fr. Luis Caetano de Souza to meet him again. This time Fr. Gonsalves told him that awards, pre-eminences and honours would be bestowed, once the natives came to power. He also pointed out to him, that in his village of Aldona there were rich and powerful persons. He asked Fr. Monis to look out for capable people who could be united into a *partido* and thereby safeguard and strengthen the project for the proposed rebellion. Fr. Monis politely declined, stating that he was a poor individual and that he and his brothers had no aspirations for honours.[22]

Salvador da Costa of Parra, who had left the *Primeiro Regimento* of the army lived in Panjim. He was invited to meet Fr. Gonsalves at the residence of Fr. Couto in the month of May 1787, in order to ferret information from him. He was asked about the state of the Praça de Rachol, whether it was in ruins and the number of whites stationed there. To this he responded that the said Praça was in good condition and that thirty whites were housed there.[23] He was also asked details about the manner in which the *Chifardes dos Granadeiros* could be seized. His response was that it was impossible to do this.[24]

In the same month of May while in Panjim, Salvador da Costa happened to meet Fr. Diego Caetano de Couto who began to make enquiries about the number of Portuguese soldiers in the *Primeiro Regimento*. To this he replied that they were 300 in number.[25]

Sebastião de Noronha, of Nagoa-Verna, a businessman, based in Panjim, was also invited to meet Fr. Gonsalves at the residence of Fr. Couto in the month of May 1787. On that occasion Fr. Gonsalves was critical of the Portuguese regime and denounced the nature of their governance.

Sebastião de Noronha continued to visit the residence of Fr. Couto on several occasions in the month of June and July, thereby revealing his deep involvement in the project. The rebel priests needed men and money but Noronha could promise to arrange only men.[26] Once he took along with him his assistant Miguel Antonio da Costa and on another occasion Bernardo de Misquita of Penha de França.[27] According to the statement of Miguel Antonio da Costa, the latter was taken to the house of Fr. Couto twice, once by Noronha and another time by Fr. Couto himself. On one of these occasions, Fr. Couto insisted that the local administration was no good. On the other occasion, Fr. Gonsalves emphasized that the enemies could easily seize his

(Miguel's) ship because there was no justice and proper system in the *Estado*, that the administrative picture was far from rosy. He stated that there was the need for a Parliament. He further said that the people of Goa were ready to rise. These *praticas* with Miguel Antonio da Costa at the home of Fr. Couto took place before the Feast of São João (June 24, 1787).[28]

Caetano Xavier da Costa, brother of Miguel served under Marechal de Campo, Francisco Antonio da Viega Coutinho. On one occasion Fr. Couto and his brother Fr. Diego happened to meet Caetano Xavier da Costa. He was led to their house, which was in the vicinity of the home of Caetano's brother Miguel. Fr. Couto began to enquire about the post he occupied. When he said that he was *Cabo da Esquadra*, the said priest responded, that shortly he would become an *official mayor*. Fr. Couto told Caetano that soon the natives would be staging a revolt to throw out the Portuguese and seize the Government of the *Estado*. The Portuguese were preoccupied with war in Europe and would be in no position to maintain their territories in Asia simultaneously.[29]

When Fr. Couto spoke to Caetano Xavier da Costa about the revolt, he began to enquire about the military strength of the Praça de Rachol. To this Caetano replied that there were about 1000 men stationed there. Fr. Couto doubted this figure and asked him to prepare a sketch of the fortification and garrison.[30]

Towards the end of June 1787, Fr. Couto spoke to the two brothers Caetano and Miguel in the presence of his brother Fr. Diego. Caetano was persuaded to get hold of the Marechal de Campo to join the movement. The former promised to do whatever he could.[31]

At the residence of Fr. Couto, other individuals were also seen. One of them was José Monteiro, resident of Santa Ignes, who lived in the coconut grove belonging to Agostinho de Mello.

He was said to have dealings with the French Company and would go on voyage from time to time.[32]

On one occasion in May, José Monteiro was a guest in the house of Fr. Couto at Panjim. Fr. Gonsalves informed him that he desired to celebrate the Feast of S. Antonio. Fr. Couto stated that the feast they were referring to was a *bulha* (fight) with the Portuguese and sought Monteiro's help. He told them that he would consult a friend and accordingly decide. Perhaps the intention then of the rebels was to hold the revolt on the Feast of S. Antonio. But Monteiro was advised by his friend not to get involved in this matter and therefore when he was called again by Fr. Couto, he declined to go.[33]

Another individual seen at the home of Fr. Couto at Panjim was Pascoal Lazaro of Santa Cruz, who was engaged in the distillation of liquor. According to Fr. Luis Caetano de Souza, Pascoal had several talks in secrecy with Fr. Couto and therefore he felt that he had joined the rebels in their plans to stage the revolt in Goa.[34] Lazaro himself in his statement confessed that he sometimes went to the house of Fr. Couto to visit his father. It was only on one such occasion that he spoke to Fr. Couto, who told him that he wished to celebrate the Feast of Santa Anna and asked him to arrange and organise the dance called 'Santa Elena'. Lazaro further stated that he did not do anything about it, nor was the feast celebrated by Fr. Couto.[35] In all probability, the rebels might have planned to use Lazaro's assistance to prepare a *bebida* (drink) that would intoxicate the Portuguese troops on the scheduled day. Again it appears that perhaps the rebels were planning to stage the revolt on the Feast of Santa Anna.

Another *assemblea* was held at the home of Fr. Couto in the month of July on the occasion of the *Concurso das Igrejas*. Fr. Caetano da Silva, Vicar of S. Lourenço de Linhares, Fr. Gonsalves, Fr. Couto and his brother Diego Caetano de Couto attended the same. The future rebellion was discussed.[36]

Fr. Luis Caetano de Souza, who lived in the vicinity of the home of Fr. Couto, besides informing the authorities in his statement during the trial about those whom he saw speaking in secrecy with the rebel priests like Fr. Monis, Pascoal Lazaro and José Monteiro, had an interesting episode to narrate. Once when he had visited Fr. Couto in March 1787, he happened to see a *rota* (rod) in a corner of the house. He remarked that it belonged to the Archbishop of Craganore. Fr. Gonsalves rebutted this saying "It does not belong to your father. It is the *rota* of a General" Fr. Luis Caetano retaliated saying "You are *General de Panelas*". This exchange of words took place in the presence of Fr. Couto. On another day, Fr. Gonsalves verbally attacked Fr. de Souza saying "You had called me *General de Panelas*, I shall seize Rarim and also Piro" Fr. de Souza pondered over these words and thought it was wrong to have such thoughts, as the Portuguese had given them happiness, had baptised them and filled them with fortune.[37]

Pilerne

The main centre for the *assembleas* was undoubtedly the Parochial House attached to the church of Pilerne. Here reunions were held on different occasions in the month of July 1787. They were usually attended by Fr. Gonsalves, Fr. Couto, Fr. Caetano da Silva, Fr. João Baptista Pinto, Fr. Miguel Alvares, Vicar of Pilerne, Fr. José Manoel Ribeiro and the Italian José Luis Guinete. Others too joined in when called. The rebels would remain there as guests for even 7 to 8 days sometimes more and would engage in *praticas* on the current scenario and the future of Goa.[38] They would be critical of the Portuguese administration, particularly the role of the Archbishop and the Governor General, who used to convey false information about the natives of Goa to the Crown. The episode of the audience of Fr. Faria with Secretario, Martinho de Melo e Castro was stressed at one of the *praticas*. The manner in which it was described, scandalised Fr. Filipe Pinto and Fr. Bernadino Ribeiro who walked out.[39]

One of the *assembleas* was held on the occasion of the Feast of S. João. The gathering included Fr. Gonsalves, Fr. Coutc, Fr. João Baptista Pinto, the Vicar Fr. Miguel Alvares, Fr. José Manoel Ribeiro and the Italian José Luis Guinete.[40]

For another conference the rebel priests had invited Tenente Nicolao Luis da Costa of the Legion of Bardez. Fr. João Baptista Pinto was in Saligão for the Feast of Santissimo Trinidade. From there he wrote some letters to Tenente Costa requesting him to meet him. On an appointed day Tenente Costa appeared at the house of Filipe Carlos de Ribeiro at Parra and from there he moved to Saligão. Both Fr. Pinto and Tenente Costa then proceeded to the church of Pilerne where they met Fr. Gonsalves. Fr. Pinto and Tenente Costa spent the night at the Parochial House at Pilerne undoubtedly discussing about the revolt that was being planned.[41]

When Fr. Miguel Alvares was questioned about the presence of Tenente Costa at his Parochial residence, he stated that the latter had come in the company of Fr. Pinto to discuss the matter of *partilhas*.[42]

According to Fr. João Baptista Pinto when interrogated during the trial, on his role of taking Tenente Costa to the Parochial House at Pilerne, he stated, that Costa had written to him before the Feast of S. João enquiring as to whether his brother Tenente Manoel Caetano Pinto was at home in Candolim. He told Tenente Costa, that his brother was not at home and he had no knowledge whether he would come for the Feasts of S. João and S. Pedro.[43] However he told Costa that he was free to come over and spend a few days, whenever he wanted.

Fr. Pinto said further that some days later when he was in Saligão, Tenente Costa had come in search of a carpenter. Fr. José Vas was there as well. They came to the Parochial House at Pilerne. On reaching there, Fr. Pinto went to rest. Therefore he did not know what had transpired between Fr. Gonsalves and Tenente Costa.[44]

Meetings and conferences were also held elsewhere in Pilerne—the residences of Fr. Vicente Alvares and Fr. José Manoel Ribeiro. The rebel priest Fr. Gonsalves was seen going for walks with José Luis Guinete from the church of Pilerne to the houses of Fr. Vicente Alvares and Fr. José Manoel Ribeiro.

On August 6, 1787 on the occasion of the Feast of Harvest, Fr. Vicente Alvares organised a dinner at his residence, to which were invited Fr. Gonsalves, Geraldo Ferreira of Arpora, Fr. José Manoel Ribeiro and Rafael Marcos.[45]

The priests would also assemble at times at the *pousada* of the residence of Fr. José Manoel Ribeiro. According to Rafael Marcos, Fr. Gonsalves, Fr. José Vas and Fr. Caetano da Silva were seen having dinner there on several occasions.[46]

Pomburpa

There were three major *assembleas* held at the Parochial House attached to the church of Pomburpa. Incidentally they coincided with the Feast of Candeus (February 2, 1787) the Feast of Nossa Senhora do Carmo (July, 16, 1787) and the Feast of Santa Anna i.e. at the end of July.

On the ocassion of the Feast of Candeus, Fr. Gonsalves went to Pomburpa accompanied by the above-said Italian. Both of them stayed there for about 4 to 5 days as guests of the Vicar João Alvares de Souza.[47]

Fr. Gonsalves returned back to Pompurpa a day or two before the Feast of Nossa Senhora do Carmo in the month of July. Fr. Caetano da Silva, came there from Velotim. Fr. Couto also arrived there with Sebastião de Noronha. The last two were there for a day or more and the first two, Fr. Gonsalves and Fr. da Silva moved on to Moira where they stayed for about four days.[48]

The last two priests returned to Pomburpa one of the days close to the Feast of Santa Anna. Fr. Gonsalves sent a *chito* (note) to Tenente Toscano, but did not receive any reply.[49] On the Feast day itself, Tenente Pedro Luis Gonzaga came to Pomburpa and was in a discussion with Fr. Gonsalves, Fr. da Silva and the Vicar of the church for about four to five hours. But on the same day he departed. Fr. da Silva left the next day, but Fr. Gonsalves remained there for two or more days.[50]

Moira

On one of the days of the Novena of Nossa Ṣenhora do Carmo in July 1787, Fr. Gonsalves and Fr. da Silva stayed for about four days perhaps from July 14 to July 18, 1787 at the Parochial House of the church of Moira, . Here they interacted with the Vicar of Moira, Filipe Antonio Vas. Over here also came Tenente Toscano and Tenente Costa. These two spent the night at Moira. Fr. Pedro Caetano José Lobo, Vicar of Tivim in his statement said that he was told by the Mestre of the church, that they were in conversation the whole night or that they did not sleep at all.[51]

As indicated earlier, Fr. Gonsalves used the method of personal meetings to get support and assistance for the cause of the revolt. The meeting organised at Moira is one such glaring example.[52]

Tivim

On perhaps July 18, 1787, Fr. Gonsalves, Fr. da Silva, Fr. Lobo, Vicar of the church of Tivim, the Curate of the said church, and Tomas Antonio Pereira, *Escrivão* of Tivim were present at the Parochial House attached to the church. It was at the time of the Novenas of S. Christopher and Santa Anna.[53]

The rebel priests Fr. da Silva and Fr. Gonsalves stood up to advocate the proposed revolt. Fr. Lobo scolded them for what he thought was too provocative and criminal, and pointed out that it was far-fetched and that they would face difficulties. In defence the said rebel priests explained in detail the plans and strategies that were going to be adopted. They spared no efforts to allay the fears and doubts of the said Vicar. They continuously assured him that every detail was taken care of and that there was no fear of failure. But they still found themselves at odds with Fr. Lobo, who was not convinced, who still offered resistance and tried to dissuade them from going ahead with the proposed rebellion.[54]

It was at Tivim that Fr. Gonsalves emphasized that the *Estado* pertained to *Igreja Grega* (Greek Church) and that priests could marry. This, the Vicar felt was a serious matter.[55]

The rebel priests separately tried to involve the Curate Fr. Baltazar Rodrigues in their movement, saying that they wished to tell him a secret.

When Fr. Gonsalves noted that Fr. Lobo was firm and that he could be a troublemaker, he sent a note to the Tenentes Toscano and Costa not to disclose the matters discussed with them to anyone and this note he read out before Fr. Lobo and the others.[56]

Velotim, Sirula

It appears that Fr. Gonsalves and Fr. da Silva visited the house of Fr. Caetano Antonio Lobo at Sirula on two occasions and that on one occasion they spent the night there. Fr. Caetano Antonio Lobo was Vicar of Reys Magos. He had come home to help his nephew José Caetano Lobo who was quite ill.[57]

While at Sirula, the above said rebels had talks with the said Vicar and his nephews José Caetano Lobo and Avelino Lourenço Lobo. Perhaps this was on July 19 or 20, 1787 after the Feast of Nossa Senhora do Carmo. He spoke about many matters that occurred in Europe, particularly Portugal. There was much talk about posts and positions.[58]

Fr. Gonsalves privately engaged himself in a conversation with Avelino Lourenço Lobo. He said "Why do we want this rule to continue in Goa? Why do we want to die? Do we have hope for advancement? It would be better if we could throw out the Portuguese and become rulers of the land". Avelino Lobo was taken aback by such statements. The latter asked Fr. Gonsalves as to how this was possible. To this the priest replied that they had the capacity.[59]

Other one-to-one personal meetings were held in Ribandar, Saligão, Aldona, Anjuna, Penha de França and Mandur.

Ribandar

Fr. Gonsalves had spoken to Fr. Pedro Dalgado in the Parochial House of the church of Ribandar in January 1787 where the latter was for mission work (*missão*). He happened to meet Fr. Gonsalves again at Piedade in the month of February where once again he had gone for mission work. Perhaps they discussed about the revolt, but when questioned, Fr. Dalgado categorically denied it.[60]

Saligão

Fr. João Baptista Pinto had gone to Saligão on the occasion of the Feast of Santissmo Trinidade. His brother-in-law Manoel Pinto, was an influential person in the village, who wielded the good will, confidence and control over the people. Apart from other reasons, Fr. Pinto met him in order to get support and financial assistance for the proposed rebellion.[61]

Mandur

In the month of July, Fr. Couto had gone to Mandur to the residence of Inacio Caetano Lopes of the Legion of Ponda. He spelt out the plans to overthrow the Portuguese rule in Goa and asked him to join this cause. Lopes showed no response.

In the month of August, Tenente Gonzaga approached Lopes seeking his help for the rebellion. He told him that once the forces would move towards Forte de S. Thiago, he and his *companhia* should join in. Gonzaga stated that unless Lopes did so, they could not proceed with the project. Lopes enquired as to when the revolt was expected to take place. To this Gonzaga replied that it would perhaps be on the day of San Lourenço (August 10).[62]

Tenente Gonzaga met Lopes on the day of the Feast of Mandur at the home of Gonzaga's friend. There were about 25 persons gathered there, most of whom were Brahmin by origin. This is according to the statement of João Vas, Soldado of the Legion of Ponda, who had accompanied Gonzaga.[63]

Aldona

On July 4, 1787, Fr. José Vas of Anjuna accompanied by Tenente Toscano, went to meet Fr. Vicente Filipe Coutinho of Aldona. As Fr. Vas was not acquainted with the latter, he requested Toscano to introduce him to Fr. Coutinho. There was a discussion about the plot hatched against the Portuguese rule. But Fr. Coutinho questioned Fr. Vas as to how it would be possible to accomplish the proposed revolt.[64]

On July 9 or 10, 1787, Fr. Gonsalves and others met the brother of Fr. Vicente Filipe Coutinho, namely Fr. Paulo Benedito on the *prayas de Velotim*. They were enquiring as to whether Fr. Coutinho was at home. They did not disclose anything to him. Fr. Paulo Benedicto was therefore confused about the whole matter. Fr. Coutinho later told his brother about his interaction with Fr. José Vas and Tenente Toscano.[65]

Anjuna

Fr. José Antonio Vas in the beginning of July received a letter from Fr. Gonsalves asking him to meet him at the Parochial House at Anjuna, where he was a guest. Accordingly, Fr. Vas went there. Fr. Gonsalves declared that they (rebels) planned to stage a revolt to free the natives from the Portuguese rule and for this purpose they had succeeded in roping in the natives who served in the Legions. In his statement Fr. Vas expressed that his reaction was that this was illicit and impossible.[66] It may be noted here that Fr. Vas had in fact served as a messenger for the rebels

Penha de França

Fr. Caetano da Silva had gone to the Parochial House of Penha de França. As it was late he requested the Curate Fr. Daniel de Albuquerque for some acomodation for the night. In the course of conversation Fr. da Silva asked the Curate if he could arrange some *balões* (vessels) and that he would intimate to him when they would be needed. The Curate replied that he would do whatever he could.[67]

Ponda

Manoel Antonio de Oliveira Pontes, *Capitão da Legião dos Voluntarios Reaes de Ponda*, in his statement said that he had witnessesed David Francisco Viegas, *Cirurgião-mor*, Tenente Manoel Caetano Pinto, Tenente Pedro Luis Gonzaga, Francisco Pereira, *Ajudante de Cirurgia* and Sargento Baltazar Caeiro, all from the Legion of Ponda, on several occasions gathering at the House of Fr. Manoel da Expectacão the Vicar of the church of Ponda.[68]

It will be in order here to conclude that the *assembleas* and personal meetings conducted and carried out in various parts of Bardez and Ilhas had a three-fold strategy. Firstly, there was an attempt to acquaint as many people as far as possible in secrecy about the revolt, to elicit their interest and enlist their participation and support. Secondly, assistance was required in terms of men and money. Without the military forces it would be impossible to carry out the plans. Thirdly, it was necessary to have a thorough knowledge of the military strength of the Government—knowledge of the fortifications and the garrisons stationed in Goa. It was necessary to know how best to attack the forts and other focal points, so as to set the stage for the revolt and ascertain its success.

A lion's share of the credit for the assemblies goes to Fr. Gonsalves, who used the churches as gathering points, moved from one village to another, for months together, almost like a man possessed, to bring his vision to fruition.

REFERENCES

1. AHU: *MI* Maço 155(153), Devassa, Auto No. 5, Statement of Fr. João Alvares de Souza.
2. AHU: *MI* Maço 155(153), Devassa Auto No. 3, Statement of Fr. Caetano da Silva, Auto No. 8, Statement of Fr. Miguel Alvares; Witness No. 7, Statement of Fr. Pedro Caetano José Lobo.
3. AHU: *MI* Maço 155(153), Devassa, Auto No. 5, Statement of Fr. João Alvares de Souza.
4. AHU: *MI* Maço 155(153), doc. dtd. 18 Aug. 1787.
5. AHU: *MI* Maço 155(153), Devassa, Auto No. 2, Statement of José Luis Guinete.
6. AHU: *MI* Maço 155(153), Devassa, Statement of Fr. Inacio Monis.
7. AHU: *MI* Maço 155(153), doc. dtd. 26 Sept. 1787.
8. AHU: *MI* Maço 155(153), doc. dtd. 18 Aug. 1787.
9. AHU: *MI* Maço 155(153), doc. dtd. 15 Dec. 1787.
10. AHU: *MI* Maço 155(153), Devassa, Auto No. 3, Statement of Fr. Caetano da Silva.
11. AHU: *MI* Maço 155(153), docs. dtd. 18 Aug. 1787; 26 Sept. 1787.
12. AHU: *MI* Maço 155(153), doc. dtd. 15 Dec. 1787.
13. AHU: *MI* Maço 155(153), doc. dtd. 15 Dec. 1787.
14. AHU: *MI* Maço 155(153), doc. dtd. 26 Sept. 1787.
15. AHU: *MI* Maço 155(153), doc. dtd. 26 Sept. 1787.
16. AHU: *MI* Maço 155(153), Devassa, Auto No. 22, Statement of Fr. João Baptista Pinto.

17. AHU: *MI* Maço 155(153), Testemunha Referida, Statement of Fr. Mestre Filipe de Melo.
18. AHU: *MI* Maço 155(153), Devassa, Auto No. 36, Statement of Fr. Diego Benedicto Lobo.
19. AHU: *MI* Maço 155(153), doc. dtd. 18 Aug. 1787.
20. AHU: *MI* Maço 155(153), Devassa, Auto No. 13, Statement of Fr. Luis Antonio Gonsalves.
21. AHU: *MI* Maço 155(153), doc. dtd 26 Sept. 1787; Devassa, Auto No.29, Statement of Sebastião de Noronha.
22. AHU: *MI* Maço 155(153), Devassa, Witness No. 9, Statement of Fr. Vicente Coutinho; Witness No. 10, Statement of Fr. Inacio Xavier Monis.
23. AHU: *MI* Maço 155(153), Devassa, Auto No. 21, Statement of Salvador da Costa.
24. AHU: *MI* Maço 155(153), Devassa, Auto No. 21, Statement of Salvador da Costa.
25. AHU: *MI* Maço 155(153), Devassa, Auto No. 21, Statement of Salvador da Costa.
26. AHU: *MI* Maço 155(153), Devassa, Auto No. 29, Statement of Sebastiao de Noronha; Witness No. 40, Statement of Caetano de Couto.
27. AHU: *MI* Maço 155(153), Devassa, Auto No. 31, Statement of Bernard de Misquita; Auto No. 45, Statement of Miguel Antonio da Costa;
28. AHU: *MI* Maço 155(153), Devassa, Auto No. 45, Statement of Miguel Antonio da Costa.
29. AHU: *MI* Maço 155(153), Devassa, Auto No. 44, Statement of Caetano Xavier da Costa.
30. AHU: *MI* Maço 155(153), Devassa, Auto No. 44, Statement of Caetano Xavier da Costa.
31. AHU: *MI* Maço 155(153), doc. dtd. 26 Sept. 1787.
32. AHU: *MI* Maço 155(153), Devassa, Auto No. 18, Statement of Fr. Luis Caetano de Souza.
33. AHU: *MI* Maço 155(153), Devassa, 32, Statement of José Monteiro
34. AHU: *MI* Maço 155(153), Devassa, Auto No. 18, Statement of Fr. Luis Caetano de Souza.
35. AHU: *MI* Maço 155(153), Devassa, Auto No. 33, Statement of Pascoal Lazaro.
36. AHU: *MI* Maço 155(153), doc. dtd. 26 Sept. 1787.
37. AHU: *MI* Maço 155(153), Devassa, Auto No. 18, Statement of Fr. Luis Caetano de Souza.
38. AHU: *MI* Maço 155(153), Devassa, Witness 11, Statement of Caetano Correa; Witness 15, Statement of Miguel de Souza.
39. AHU: *MI* Maço 155(153), Devassa, Witness 14, Statement of Tomas Filipe Ribeiro.
40. AHU: *MI* Maço 155(153), Devassa, Referimento of Witness No. 7, Statement of Fr. Pedro Caetano José Lobo.
41. AHU: *MI* Maço 155(153), Devassa, Witness 14, Statement of Tomas Filipe Ribeiro;Witness No. 33, Statement of Fr. Rafael Marcos.

42. AHU: *MI* Maço 155(153), Devassa, Auto No.8, Statement of Fr. Miguel Alvares.

43. AHU: *MI* Maço 155(153), Devassa, Auto No. 22, Statement of Fr. João Baptista Pinto.

44. AHU: *MI* Maço 155(153), Devassa, Auto No. 22, Statement of Fr. João Baptista Pinto.

45. AHU: *MI* Maço 155(153), Devassa, Testemunha Referida, Statement of Geraldo Ferreira.

46. AHU: *MI* Maço 155(153), Devassa, Witness No. 33, Statement of Fr. Rafael Marcos.

47. AHU: *MI* Maço 155(153), Devassa, Witness No. 12, Statement of Caetano Mestre.

48. AHU: *MI* Maço 155(153), Devassa, Witness No. 12, Statement of Caetano Mestre.

49. AHU: *MI* Maço 155(153), Devassa, Witness No. 12, Statement of Caetano Mestre.

50. AHU: *MI* Maço 155(153), Devassa, Witness No. 12, Statement of Caetano Mestre; Witness No. 13, Statement of Andre Borges.

51. AHU: *MI* Maço 155(153), Devassa, Witness No.7, Statement of Fr. Pedro Caetano José Lobo; Witness No. 34, Statement of Antonio Filisberto da Silva; Witness No. 35, Statement of Francisco Pereira; Witness No. 37, Statement of Pedro Feriaz (?) Witness No. 39, Statement of Fr. Pedro de Souza.

52. AHU: *MI* Maço 155(153), Devassa, Auto No. 6, Statement of Tenente Inacio Caetano Toscano; undtd. Statement of Tenente Inacio Caetano Toscano; Denunciation of Tenente Nicolao Luis da Costa.

53. AHU: *MI* Maço 155(153), Devassa, Testemunha Referida, Statement of Tomas Antonio Pereira.

54. AHU: *MI* Maço 155(153), Devassa, Witness No. 7, Statement of Fr. Pedro Caetano José Lobo; Witness No. 8, Statement of Fr. Baltazar Rodrigues.

55. AHU: *MI* Maço 155(153), Devassa, Witness No. 7, Statement of Fr. Pedro Caetano José Lobo.

56. AHU: *MI* Maço 155(153) Devassa, Witness No. 7, Statement of Fr. Pedro Caetano José Lobo; Witness No. 8, Fr. Baltazar Rodrigues.

57. AHU: *MI* Maço 155(153), Devassa, Testemunha Referida, Statement of José Caetano Lobo.

58. AHU: *MI* Maço 155(153), Devassa, Testemunha Referida, No. 7, Statement of Fr. Caetano Antonio Lobo.

59. AHU: *MI* Maço 155(153), Devassa, Statement of Avelino Lourenço Lobo.

60. AHU: *MI* Maço 155(153), Devassa, Auto No. 41, Statement of Fr. Pedro Dalgado.

61. AHU: *MI* Maço 155(153), Devassa, Auto No. 31, Statement of Manoel Pinto.

62. AHU: *MI* Maço 155(153), Devassa, Auto No. 34, Statement of Inacio Caetano Lopes.

63. AHU: *MI* Maço 155(153), Devassa, Auto No. 23, Statement of João Vas.

64. AHU: *MI* Maço 155(153), Devassa, Witness No. 9, Statement of Fr. Vicente Filipe Coutinho.
65. AHU: *MI* Maço 155(153), Devassa, Witness No. 9, Statement of Fr. Vicente Filipe Coutinho.
66. AHU: *MI* Maço 155(153), Devassa, Auto No. 20, Statement of Fr. José Antonio Vas.
67. AHU: *MI* Maço 155(153), doc. dtd. 18 Aug. 1787; Statement of Fr. Daniel de Albuquerque.
68. AHU: *MI* Maço 155(153), Devassa, Testemunha Referida, Statement of Manoel Antonio de Oliveira Pontes.

5

PLOTTING AND PLANNING : MEN, MONEY AND OTHER STRATEGIES

This chapter tends to explore the other approaches and strategies that the rebels set their minds on, for without logistic support, their project was doomed to failure.

Military to the Fore

It needs to be noted that there was connivance with the military. In the Legion of Ponda, Tenente Pedro Luis Gonzaga and Tenente Manoel Caetano Pinto supported the effort. They were entrusted with the task of attracting as many natives in their Legion to the cause of the intended rebellion. Five of the nine *companhias* of the Legion had pledged their support. Native *soldados, sargentos, cabos, furreis* etc. were drawn in. The *Devassa* records mention the names of Sargento Baltazar Caeiro, Cabo Manoel Ferrão, Cabo Caetano da Costa, Cabo Antonio Fernandes *Cirurgião - mor* David Viegas, *Ajudante de Cirurgia* Françisco Pereira, Inacio Caetano Lopes and others.

As regards the Legion of Bardez, the rebels had the support of Tenente Inacio Caetano Toscano and Tenente Nicolao

Luis da Costa. Both had to win over the forces under them, so that along with the Legion of Ponda they would raise the banner of revolt against the Portuguese. Both the Tenentes attended meetings summoned by the rebel priests. Of signifance was the one held at Moira around mid-July. Costa was also seen at Pilerne. Fr. José Vas promised Toscano, that money to the tune of 4000 *xerafins* would be provided to lure the natives in his Legion to join the movement.[1]

It needs to be emphasized that Tenente Gonzaga's contribution towards winning support and whipping up emotions in the Legion of Ponda, is commendable. He tried to win the forces over, through close interplay and personal empathy. He would use some pretext or other to speak to his subordinates. His interactions and meetings with them prove it.[2] It would not be out of order to examine them in detail.

In his statement David Francisco Viegas indicated, that on July 12 or 13, 1787 Tenente Gonzaga came to his *Quartel* and called him out. At first he found his words "*Vamos nos dar um cassada nos Portuguezes*" frivolous. But on second thoughts he was shocked and scandalised.

In fact the spirit and disposition of Viegas underwent change. According to him the Legion of Ponda, by the end of July or the beginning of August, 1787 was gripped with the spirit of rebellion.[3]

Sargento Baltazar Caeiro made matters clear that Tenente Gonzaga and Tenente Manoel Caetano Pinto requested him to arrange 200 men in his native place Assolna, for in that village there were sturdy men available, capable of dealing with the Portuguese.[4]

Tenente Gonzaga had also spoken to Francisco Pereira, *Ajudante de Cirurgia* about the revolt. The former told the latter that the Portuguese called them *cachorros*, *negros* and *carastros* and for this humiliation, some natives planned to stage a revolt, clamouring for liberation.[5]

Gonzaga on one occasion told Cabo Manoel Ferrão that they (rebels) were going to kill the Portuguese. Some days later the said Tenente called Ferrão to his *Quartel* to cut some bamboo roots. He ordered the latter to take a pledge not to disclose to anyone what was being planned. He said that six legions would be created, against which they would be promoted as per their merit. He said further that the whole of the Legion of Bardez and a part of the Legion of Ponda were ready to join the movement. On August 5, 1787 Gonzaga promised to make Ferrão an *Alferes*.[6]

João Vas, Soldado in the said Legion of Ponda was once accosted by Gonzaga (August 2, 1787), who said "Would it not be better to be rulers of this land. For this end, we have to throw out the Portuguese". Vas asked him how this was possible. His response was that they would do so with the help of the Bhonsles. Vas disclosed this interaction to Cabo Manoel Ferrão the next day. The said Cabo told him that the Tenente had also spoken to him on the matter.[7]

Caetano da Costa, Cabo da Esquadra on one occasion in June, when he went to Ponda, happened to meet Tenente Gonzaga and they had a discussion with him on the proposed rebellion.[8]

Tenente Gonzaga on the occasion of the Feast of Mandur met Inacio Caetano Lopes. He sought the help and co-operation of Lopes and his *companhia*, without which he felt the rebels could not go ahead with the proposed revolt.[9]

Besides Tenente Gonzaga, the efforts of David Francisco Viegas needs to be remembered. At the end of July, Viegas called Cabo Antonio Fernandes outside the *Guarda* and told him that soon Goa would be theirs and the Portuguese would no longer rule over them. Everything was planned and arranged for, outside the army. Almost everyone from within the Legion of Ponda was ready. Only four *companhias* were not ready to join. He said "For now we are not required to do anything. Do not speak to anyone about this." He said further that he had singled him out, to tell him all this, as the other *Cabos* were not capable of speaking to their subordinates to convince them to join the movement for the revolt. However there was time for all this. Some days later Viegas sent a message to Fernandes not to disclose what was discussed, with anyone.[10]

In addition, individual efforts were made to lure officers and officials of the military forces to join the cause. For instance, Fr. Jorge stated that he had invited another Cabo who was a resident of Volvoi.[11] Manoel Luis of Candolim, brother-in-law of Fr. Couto, was told by the latter to draw in his nephews, who were soldiers of the *Primeiro Regimento* to the cause of the future revolt. It was also planned to target Narba Naique and Rogu Saunto to join with their *Partidos de Sipais*.[12]

Other Armed Assistance

Sebastião de Noronha was a businessman from Verna-Nagoa, who had a residence at Panjim. He conducted business in the South.

The rebels got in touch with him, convinced him to join the movement for the revolt and arrange men for the purpose. He was seen at the residence of Fr. Couto at Panjim and at the *assembleas* at Piedade and Pomburpa.

Noronha had a *correspondente* at Assolna, namely João de Souza Onorcar, who also conducted business in the South. Noronha went to Assolna and asked him to arrange some good sailors for his ship, about 25 to 50 of them. When Onorcar enquired as to why he needed so many men, Noronha replied that he needed the same for another ship which he employed for freighting purposes.

Noronha did not specify the quality of the men required nor the place from which they needed to be drawn.[13] On another occasion when Onorcar was in Panjim, he happened to meet Noronha, who once again requested him to arrange some men.[14]

Noronha had in fact even gone to Penha de França to meet Bernardo de Misquita to ask him to arrange men for Fr. Couto.[15]

But the statement of Fr. Gonsalves, that due to the efforts of Noronha, 800 to 1000 men were arranged from Cuncolim and soon this number would swell, does not seem acceptable. The rebels claimed that they not only had an ample supply of men from Cuncolim but also from various parts of the Province of Bardez specially Siolim.[16]

Fr. Gonsalves had written to Fr. José Ribeiro who was at Pune to arrange some men from the Maratha dominions to come to the assistance of the rebels on the scheduled day. It was also strategised to speak to Francisco de Souza commonly known as Francisco Gancar, who for sometime served as *Cabo de Partidos* and he was at this point of time a resident of Pirne, to arrange an agent who could from the villages beyond the walls of Bardez, arrange 100 Muslims for which they would be paid and who could be sheltered in the church of Pomburpa. Fr. Gonsalves also requested Fr. Lobo to get the help of the people of Assonora, which was under his jurisdiction. He could draw them through his devotion and also by making requisite promises for their advancement.[17]

Fr. David de Albuquerque, Curate of the church of Penha de França was entrusted with the task of arranging *balões* for the scheduled date of the revolt.[18]

Fr. Gonsalves had stated on one occasion, that through the intervention of a certain person, he had obtained the support of the people of Cumbarjua for the intended revolt.[19]

The rebels indicated that they would get the help of the Emperor of Germany who would send two ships with 500 men. Moreover, the natives of Germany residing in Goa, would participate in the revolt.[20] This was indeed a crucial determinant. It was also stated that two ships of an empire that had *feitorias* on the west coast would come to their assistance and that the same power would also help with money. This was discussed on July 18, 1787 at Tivim, in the presence of the Vicar, Fr. Pedro Caetano José Lobo and others.

It was also said that six ships of a nation were expected, that a *nau* served by 300 to 400 persons would arrive, that 1000 men would come from outside the *Estado*, specially 200 Muslims.[21]

Money Matters

Hamstrung by financial constraints and stringency, efforts were made by the rebels to raise funds. This is evident from the contacts they made with Sebastião de Noronha. At Piedade he was asked to arrange men and money. He replied that he could not render help relating to money. Perhaps the rebels also planned to rope in Rama Sinay, a well-known businessman of Panjim, who had business dealings with Onorcar.

The rebel priests had meetings with José Monteiro, another businessman who was invited to join the conspiracy for the revolt. Fr. Gonsalves while at Cochin had met Monteiro.[22]

On one occasion, when he was at Panjim, Fr. Diego Caetano de Couto came to call José Monteiro on behalf of Fr. Gonsalves and had made a strange statement that Monteiro must be in the possession of much money.[23]

The rebel priests, Fr. Gonsalves and Fr. da Silva, while at Tivim kept saying that they had many offers of money, that many natives were ready to finance the project.[24] Fr. José Vas mentioned to Tenente Toscano that several persons from Ilhas had offered requisite money to accomplish the success of the impending revolt.[25] He further stated that a person from Piedade had offered 16,000 *xerafins.*[26] Manoel Pinto promised to use his influence and power to acquire finance. It was believed that the rebels had 30,000 to 40,000 *xerafins*.

Help from Indian Rulers

Fr. Gonsalves did attempt to get the help of the Indian rulers specially of the South. The rebels spoke of getting assistance from Tipu Sultan, the Bhonsles, the Marathas, the King of Travancore and the King of Sunda, in order to successfully stage a revolt against the Portuguese regime.[27] Any one of them would have been an extremely useful ally. But at the same time the rebels could be totally unfounded by the unreliability of their support.

Relating to the Bhonsles, Fr. Gonsalves described them as people with courage whom the Portuguese feared. There were also talks of integrating the *Estado da India* into Bhonsle territories. It was also said that if the King of Sunda became a Christian, they would offer the government to him.[28]

The *Devassa* records are vague on the issue of external intervention. In fact there are no detailed and clear-cut plans drawn up. It does not seem possible for the rebels to get the support of the Sunda ruler, as he had been deposed, deprived of his lands and was under Portuguese protection and shelter. The Bhonsles by a pact were at truce with the Portuguese. The Marathas were pre-occupied with their war with Tipu Sultan to be bothered with Goa. This leaves us with Tipu Sultan.

According to Cunha Rivara, Tipu Sultan was the axis round which the rebels revolved. They pinned their hopes on him. He was of the opinion that Tipu Sultan was eager to occupy Goa and that perhaps there was an understanding between the rebels and

Tipu.[29] The rebels would first break out in revolt, and then call upon Tipu to help them. But some studies have been carried out relating to this. It has been conclusively proven that Tipu's designs on Goa in 1787 were not fact but fiction.[30]

Other Strategies

Vis-à-vis plans and strategies described above, the role of the Vicars in their respective parishes was established by the rebels as crucial, in the proposed rebellion. They could incite and influence the masses and spread the flame of revolt within their parish and from one parish to another in the *arcebispado*.[31]

The rebels decided to use the Vicars because they were well-aware that they wielded authority and could extract obedience from their parishfolk. Their passionate and high-pitched announcements would make the requisite impact.

It was certain that the rebels intended to make their first moves with the Legion of Ponda. It was in all likelihood that Fr. Manoel da Expectação, the Vicar of the church of Ponda was told that on the day of the revolt, to instigate the people of his parish to join hands with the Legion of Ponda.[32]

Word was also spread, that one night the British Americans (American Revolution), had taken refuge in the churches under parish priests, and had got together to free themselves from the British yoke. It was decided to stage the revolt in Goa on the same lines. Firstly, the priests would be sent notices. They would arrange to ring the bells of their churches on the fixed day, to assemble the people, read letters, including that of Fr. Caetano Vitorino de Faria to convince the people to unite, to bring an end to the Portuguese rule in Goa.[33]

As a method to intimate, to inform, to confirm and to remind about the details of the plot, what needed to be done, etc. secret messages (*recados*) in the form of notes (*chitos*) were sent through a *portador* to the rebels. Secrecy was maintained at all costs and therefore the messages were brief and sometimes in code language. One such *recado* was sent to Fr. Pedro José Cardozo, Vicar of Socorro by his nephew to come to Pilerne. It stated that "Senhor Guinete and Luis Tio would like to speak to you". He also wrote that there was a vessel for him to come to Piedade. He was required to send his response through the *portador*.[34]

Fr. José Vas had passed on many messages on behalf of Fr. Gonsalves and Fr. Pinto about the said conspiracy. He served as the messenger or the carrier of messages, some of which were for awareness, some to remind about the works to be done and others to pospone or even stop the execution of works. But all this was denied by Fr. Vas.[35]

It was also planned to influence, even bribe the bakers to poison the bread to end the lives of the whites, specially white soldiers who served for the defence of the *Estado*.[36] This would be carried out on the day fixed for the rebellion. The rebels had a recipe for a special drink with which the soldiers would be inebriated and unconscious for a period of about five days.[37] The plan was to adminster the drink to five hundred Portuguese.[38]

From the above discussion, the progress of the plot is clear. The rebels declared that the whole of Bardez, Ilhas and Salcette were in a state of readiness with men, money and ammunition to stage the revolt to overthrow the Portuguese rule in Goa, to throw them out of India and even to kill them. Fr. Gonsalves categorically said "All anticipated matters have been dealt with".[39] But there is no denying of the fact that there were problems and complexities that the rebels faced and were bound to face as they moved along.

REFERENCES

1. AHU: *MI* Maço 155(153), Devassa, Denunciation of Fr. Vicente Filipe Coutinho.
2. AHU: *MI* Maço 155(153), Devassa, Auto No. 24, Statement of Pedro Luis Gonzaga.
3. AHU: *MI* Maço 155(153), Devassa, Auto No. 27, Statement of David Francisco Viegas.
4. AHU: *MI* Maço 155(153), Devassa, Statement of Baltazar Caeiro.
5. AHU: *MI* Maço 155(153), Devassa, Auto No. 8, Statement of Francisco Pereira.
6. AHU: *MI* Maço 155(153), Devassa, Auto No. 17, Statement of Manoel Ferrão.
7. AHU *MI* Maço 155(153), Devassa, Auto No. 23, Statement of João Vas.
8. AHU *MI* Maço 155(153), Devassa, Auto No. 44, Statement of Caetano da Costa.
9. AHU: *MI* Maço 155(153), Devassa, Auto No. 34, Statement of Inacio Caetano Lopes.
10. AHU: *MI* Maço 155(153), Devassa, Auto No. 16, Statement of Antonio Fernandes.
11. AHU: *MI* Maço 155(153), doc. dtd. 26 Sept. 1787.
12. AHU: *MI* Maço 155(153), doc. dtd. 26 Sept. 1787.
13. AHU: *MI* Maço 155(153), Devassa, Auto No. 28, Statement of João de Souza Onorcar; Auto No. 29, Statement of Sebastião de Noronha.
14. AHU: *MI* Maço 155(153), Devassa, Auto No. 28, Statement of João de Souza Onorcar.
15. AHU: *MI* Maço 155(153), Devassa, Auto No. 29, Statement of Sebastião de Noronha.
16. AHU: *MI* Maço 155(153), Denunciation of Fr. Vicente Filipe Coutinho.
17. AHU: *MI* Maço 155(153), doc. dtd. 18 Aug. 1787.
18. AHU: *MI* Maço 155(153) doc. dtd. 18 Aug. 1787.
19. AHU: *MI* Maço 155(153) doc. dtd. 26 Sept. 1787.
20. AHU: *MI* Maço 155(153), Denunciation of Fr. Vicente Filipe Coutinho; doc. dtd 15 Dec. 1787.
21. AHU: *MI* Maço 155(153), Witness No. 7, Statement of Fr. Pedro Caetano José Lobo; Auto No. 6, Statement of Inacio Caetano Toscano.
22. AHU: *MI* Maço 155(153), Devassa, Auto No. 32, Statement of José Monteiro.
23. AHU: *MI* Maço 155(153), Devassa, Auto No. 32, Statement of José Monteiro.
24. AHU: *MI* Maço 155(153), Devassa, Witness No. 7, Statement of Fr. Pedro Caetano José Lobo.
25. AHU: *MI* Maço 155(153), Devassa, Witness 9, Statement of Fr. Vicente Filipe Coutinho.

26. AHU: *MI* Maço 155(153), Devassa, Auto No. 6, Statement of Inacio Caetano Toscano.
27. AHU: *MI* Maço 155(153), Devassa, Auto No. 2, Statement of José Luis Guinete; doc. dtd. 12 Aug. 1787.
28. AHU: *MI* Maço 155(153), Devassa, Auto No. 2, Statement of José Luis Guinete; Auto No. 7, Statement of Fr. Antonio Filipe Vas; Auto No. 31, Statement of Bernardo de Mesquita; Auto No. 41, Statement of Fr. Pedro Dalgado.
29. Charles Borges ed., *Goa and the Revolt of 1787*, pp. 117-118.
30. Celsa Pinto, "Tipu Sultan's Designs on Goa: Fact or Fiction". *Goa: Images and Perceptions. Studies in Goan History*, 1996, Goa, pp. 21-23; Ernestina Carreira, "Goa in the Reign of Tipoo Sultan. International Politics and the Pinto's Conspiracy" A paper presented at the Fifth International Seminar on Indo-Portuguese History, Cochin, Jan. 1989.
31. AHU: *MI* Maço 155(153), Statement of Fr. Antonio Silveira de Menezes.
32. AHU: *MI* Maço 155(153), Devassa, Auto No. 4, Statement of Fr. Manoel da Expectação.
33. AHU: *MI* Maço 155(153), Devassa, Auto No. 15, Statement of Baltazar Caeiro.
34. AHU: *MI* Maço 155(153), doc. dtd. 25 May 1787.
35. AHU: *MI* Maço 155(153), Devassa, Auto No. 20, Statement of Fr. José Vas.
36. AHU: *MI* Maço 155(153), Devassa, Statement of Antonio Silveira de Menezes.
37. AHU: *MI* Maço 155(153), Devassa, Denunciation of Fr. Vicente Filipe Coutinho; doc. dtd. 26 Sept. 1787.
38. AHU: *MI* Maço 155(153), Devassa, Statement of Inacio Caetano Toscano.
39. AHU: *MI* Maço 155(153), Devassa, Witness No. 7, Statement of Fr. Pedro Caetano José Lobo.

6

D-DAY

Plan of Action

A three-pronged plan of action was worked out by the rebels. It was felt, that it was time for a show of force.

The first was the role of armed men. A major military initiative and effort was planned. The Legion of Ponda would make a circuitous detour around the pass of the Fort of S.Thiago and lay seige to it. It would then be placed under a competent garrison. The Legion would march on and seize the Arsenal. This military strategy would be reinforced with the participation of the people in support of the rebellion. The Legion of Bardez would be directed to make movements towards the Praça d' Agoada. Fr. Caetano da Silva, Vicar of S. Lourenço and the same Praça, had to render help with a surprise attack on the said Praça.

The second was the role of the Vicar of each parish. At an assigned time he had to arrange to ring the bells of the Parish Church to gather all the people of the parish. They would unite and clamour for liberty and for better times.

The third was that the rebels had gained the good will of the bakers, who would poison the bread, that was to be distributed amongst the troops. They had prepared a drink to intoxicate the soldiers.[1]

According to Fr. Gonsalves necessary steps and precautions would be taken at the time of the execution of the project.

Details of the military action that was planned for D-Day are unfolded hereforth.

It was planned that before the *fragatas* moved out, the Legion of Ponda and the *Partido* of Narba Naique would march towards the Fort of Santiago. After seizing this fort and taking control of the ammunition stocked there, they would guard the same with some men. The troops would continue their movements and occupy the *Arsenal* and *Casa de Polvora*. They would lay their hands on whatever they could get, even from the *Cofres do Erario*, for they had succeeded in corrupting the officials of the *Fazenda*. It needs to be stressed that the *Companhia de Guarda* and the *Fazenda,* had native soldiers and officials respectively.

Two *manchuas* would be despatched, one for the frontier site at the Convent of S. Boaventura and the other for another frontier site at the *Alfandega* (Customs House)

The troops would move to Ribandar where they would bifurcate—one division for the eastern side of Ribandar and the other for the western side, i.e. at the start of Ponte de Pangim. This was designed to make quick penetrations into enemy lines.

The Legion of Bardez would march towards the Praça d' Agoada. The crowds would rally round them. They would await for an opportune moment to strike. Fr. Caetano da Silva, Vicar of S. Lourenço de Linhares and of the same Praça, would make the officials surrender.

It was further planned that at the time when the said Legions were on the march, the natives would join them with arms and *segulhos* using iron and fire against all the Portuguese they encountered Some of them would be armed with bamboo sticks to attack the whites and would shout '*viva viva*'.

Fr. Couto and Sebastião de Noronha, residents of Panjim would galvanise the people of Panjim and of the neighbouring areas to take the town by storm.[2] They would attack the *Palacio de Pangim*, the *Companhia da Guarda* of the Governor General posted at the same place and the *Regimento da Artilharia* stationed at Gaspar Dias. These were the prime targets

To facilitate all this, it was planned that the bakers would prepare bread with poison for the Portuguese forces. They had already prepared a drink for distribution amongst the soldiers so that they would be unconscious for five to seven days.

Some of them would lay in wait for the Governor General when he would move towards the *Junta da Fazenda*. They would seize him and keep him at some location for not more than a day. Other principal persons—civil, military and ecclesiastical—would also be arrested. For the arrests of the Governor General and the Archbishop, the rebels had persuaded some blacks (*cafres*) to do the work. The Governor General and the other arrested persons would be sent back to Portugal at an appropriate time.

Fr. Gonsalves stated that he had arranged for fake seals of the said Governor General, so as to issue orders as and when wanted. By one such order they would summon the Marechal from Salcette and get him arrested. Then they would order the *Companhias de Granadeiros* stationed at the Praça de Rachol to move out. They would be directed to march towards the Paço de S. Lourenço where they would be ambushed so as to create confusion.[3]

Then it was planned that steps would be taken to occupy all the other *praças* and to establish a Republic.[4] They would set up a government on the lines of that of Venice. There would be a *Superior* to head the Republic. The rebels planned to select Inacio

Pinto of Candolim to undertake this work. For the expenditure of this entire project, finance would be provided by Sebastião de Noronha. Tenente Manoel Caetano Pinto said that Manoel Pinto of Saligão had agreed to give some assistance.[5]

One can easily speculate that the above-described plan of action, if executed well, could have ended the Portuguese regime in Goa in 1787, within a day or a span of a few days. The rebels stood a fair chance of victory. It certainly appeared to be a win-win situation.

Date of the Revolt

Some historians hold the view that August 10, 1787 was the date fixed for the revolt. This stand is based on Cunha Rivara's version.[6] The latter in all probability relied on the conversation that Tenente Gonzaga had with Inacio Caetano Lopes at Mandur.

The truth is that the *Devassa* records throw up different dates. There was a discussion held in the Legion of Ponda that the rebellion would be staged between August 16 and August 20. On one occasion, Francisco Pereira was told by Tenente Gonzaga that the rebellion was planned for August 20 or sometime beyond.[7]

On August 5, Tenente Gonzaga approached Baltazar Caeiro, requesting him to arrange 200 men from his village of Assolna, men who would be capable of leading a *partido* against the Portuguese.[8] If August 10, was the date scheduled for the revolt, would it be possible that such a discussion for requirements be still on with five days to go?

It is quite obvious that the date in question kept shifting or was being postponed. The rebels wanted it to take place on and to coincide with a significant day, like the Feast of S. Antonio, or of Santanna or of S. Lourenço, perhaps because of the religious significance or because it was easier to create confusion on such a day. But in any case they were anxious to stage it before the arrival of the annual *Nau de Viagem* in September, perhaps fearing that reinforcements would arrive from Portugal.

REFERENCES

1. AHU: *MI* Maço 155(153), doc. dtd. 15 Dec. 1787.
2. AHU: *MI* Maço 155(153), doc. dtd. 26 Sept. 1787.
3. AHU: *MI* Maço 155(153), doc. dtd. 18 Aug. 1787.
4. HAG: *MR* 170A, fl. 23.
5. AHU: *MI* Maço 155(153), doc. dtd. 26 Sept. 1787.
6. Borges, ed., *Goa and the Revolt of 1787*, p. 38.
7. AHU: *MI* Maço 155(153), Devassa, Auto No. 9, Statement of Francisco Pereira.
8. AHU *MI* Maço 155(153), Devassa, Statement of Baltazar Caeiro.

7

BETRAYAL: CONSPIRACY TO DENOUNCE

History is never neat and without edges This was also with the intended revolt of 1787. There was a complete twist to the tale.

The meeting at Moira on July 15, 1787 followed by that in Tivim, on July 18, was the starting point of a series of events leading to denunciation and betrayal. While it took about one and a half years for the movement against the Portuguese to take shape, it took just one and a half months for the conspiracy to denounce, to result in actual denunciation.

The main location of the betrayal was the province of Bardez, specially, at Tivim, Aldona and the Legion of Bardez with its headquarters at Colvale. The anxieties and doubts in the mind of Tenente Inacio Toscano about the proposed rebellion and his attempts to seek advice and discuss it with others—Tenente Nicolao da Costa, Fr. Pedro Caetano José Lobo and Fr. Vicente Filipe Coutinho aroused suspicion and stirred up trouble. It confounded and compounded matters. The said priests felt threatened. It led them to tread a safe and secure path to save their own skin. In fact the last two were openly opposed to the staging of the revolt, not out of love for Portugal and the Portuguese regime but because it was felt that it was not feasible and would result in harsh reprisals.

Intially all three of them advised Toscano to keep silent over the issue and not to report or make any denunciation. In fact Fr. Lobo on one occasion said that it would be immaturish to intimate the authorities without enough proof. Fr. Coutinho on the underhand narrated an episode of a rebellion which was denounced and brought nothing but pain and punishment in its wake.

In the course of time, after gathering more details about the intended revolt, and fearing that Toscano would involve them in deep trouble, Tenente Costa, Fr. Lobo and Fr. Coutinho, without informing Tenente Toscano, made separate and individual denunciations before the authorities, that blew the lid off the boiling pot of rebellion.

The circumstances that triggered the above said developments are examined below in detail.

At the meeting at Moira on July, 15 1787, Tenente Costa and Tenente Toscano were told by Fr. Gonsalves about the steps that had been taken and those that were needed to be taken, relating to the impending revolt. This left Toscano much disturbed. He felt that there was too much risk involved and tried to convince Costa that they should report the matter. The latter told him to wait for four to five days.[1]

Meanwhile Fr. José Vas met Toscano. The latter narrated to him all that had happened at Moira. Fr. Vas who put up a veil of ignorance and innocence stated that he had no knowledge of the revolt.

Soon after this incident, Toscano planned to proceed to Aldona to pay a visit to his brother who was sick. Fr. Vas accompanied him.

In the evening of the same day, Fr. Vas turned up at the house of Toscano's brother. As he wanted a breviary, Toscano took him to Fr. Vicente Filipe Coutinho. While Fr. Vas was busy praying, Toscano torn with conflicting thoughts, spilt out the issue of the revolt to Fr. Coutinho and expressed his apprehensions. The immediate reaction of the priest was that of disbelief and that it would never be successful. He was at variance with this matter. At first he told Toscano to intimate the issue to the authorities. Later, he felt that either way things could go bad. He gave an account of a telling and interesting episode. It was about a revolt planned by two *Capitaens* and others. One of them leaked the matter to the Viceroy and he was immediately seized at the *Palacio*. The *Capitaens* were arrested, so also some natives who were involved. Some fled, some were caught and some made false statements against the accused. The *Capitaens* were executed, others were exiled and one died in prison. No natives could move about with *cabedeira* nor were they allowed to keep anything of iron at home. Fr. Coutinho very sanctimoniously requested Toscano to pray to the Five Wounds of Christ, so that whatever was planned would not be successful.[2] As Fr. Vas had finished his prayers, both closed up their conversation. But before doing so, Fr. Coutinho insisted that Toscano should not tell anyone, that he had spoken to him (Fr. Coutinho) about the intended revolt and if asked, to say that they had been discussing some other matter.

On the way back, Fr. Vas questioned Toscano about the conversation he had with Fr. Coutinho and let him know that he had overheard part of it. Toscano begged Fr. Vas to take a pledge not to disclose to anyone what he (Toscano) had told him.[3]

Toscano on the next day proceeded to Colvale and a few days later Tenente Costa received a note from Fr. Gonsalves not to go ahead with the matter he had discussed.[4]

It seems that Costa and Toscano then went to meet Fr. Lobo, who told them, that on July 18, 1787, the rebel priests Fr. Gonsalves and Fr. da Silva came to meet him. They spelt out without any reservations, the plans and strategies for the future revolt. Fr. Lobo drew out every detail from them. But the passionate defence of their plans did not go well with him.

It was at this stage that Toscano expressed that it would be better to report and be free of the rebels. Costa also felt the same way. But Fr. Lobo felt that it would be premature to do so without proof. Eventually Costa and Toscano came to an agreement that they would not inform the matter to the Coronel, nor diclose and discuss the issue with anyone. They expressed thanks to the Almighty, that they were out of the movement in which the rebels wanted to drag them.[5]

After this, both Toscano and Costa maintained secrecy for they felt that the rebels had discontinued with their plans of staging a revolt, so as not to cause harm to the public. However at the Feast of Santiago, Toscano learnt that the said rebels had resumed their operations, that Fr. Lobo knew about this and had not informed Toscano about it. Toscano therefore came to the realisation, that each one of them was playing his own game to save his skin, and that he should not hesitate to do likewise.

At the Feast of Santiago Fr. Vicente Filipe Coutinho behaved strangely. He began questioning Toscano as to what he had done or planned to do relating to the issue of the intended rebellion. Toscano told him that his brother-in-law had advised him to end the issue once and for all.[6] He therefore wanted to report the matter to the Archbishop. Fr. Coutinho responded saying that as he (Toscano) was an adult, he was at liberty to report whatever and whenever he wanted. Toscano, however observed that Fr. Coutinho was behaving in a furtive manner.He felt that the sheer fear of being caught, could make the priest capable of stabbing him in the back, by reporting everything to the authorities.[7]

Fr. Lobo, too, behaved strangely at the said Feast of Santiago. He asked Toscano as to why Fr. Vas had come. Toscano responded that he should not feign ignorance, as Fr. Vas was known to be a messenger of the rebel priests. Toscano grew suspicious as to why Fr. Lobo was questioning him in this manner and felt that perhaps he was upto no good.[8]

At the said feast, Salvador Caetano Lobo, brother of Fr. Lobo called him "*criado de Senhor Coronel*" and for about half an hour hovered around him trying to ferret from him the nature of the *officio* he would be submitting to the authorities.[9]

Toscano returned back to Colvale sick. Fr. Vas came there too. Toscano overheard the priest conspiring with Tenente Costa. In fact Fr. Vas accused Toscano of being the cause of all the trouble and vowed to speak against him. He told Costa to report against him. Toscano felt that perhaps the priest hated him because of his brother and also because he would at times call him an associate of Fr. Gonsalves.

Under the above circumstances, it was not surprising, that Tenente Toscano was convinced that he should not delay any further and should make his denunciation before the authorities at the earliest. He returned home sick and pestered his brother to arrange a vessel, so that he could move to Panjim to intimate the Governor General all that had happened with him in the past few days. He narrated to his brother how he got embroiled in the intrigue swirling around him. His brother subjected him to a tirade. Toscano informed him that he had sought the advice of Fr. Vicente Filipe Coutinho, who told him not to report anything for the moment. Besides he had spoken to Fr. Lobo and to Tenente Costa and that the latter prohibited him from speaking about it.[10]

As Tenente Toscano was ill, his brother conveyed the news of the impending revolt to the authorities at Panjim on August 5, 1787. A written denunciation could be made only the following day.

But much before Toscano could make his moves, Tenente Costa, Fr. Lobo and Fr. Coutinho did so.

Tenente Costa at first decided to be silent on the matter, as he was convinced by Fr. Lobo, that the rebel priests Fr. Gonsalves and Fr. da Silva had been dissuaded by him and that they had given up their intentions and plans to go ahead with the revolt. But when he heard on the occasion of the Feast of Santiago at Tivim that the rebels still vigorously pursued them, he changed his mind.[11]

On August 3, 1787 Toscano spoke to Costa about the matter and requested that they should make a joint denunciation. On seeing that Toscano was impeded by illness, Costa did not desire to delay any further and therefore denounced the proposed revolt before Coronel Manoel Godinho de Mira on August 4, 1787.[12] This was an act of betrayal towards a comrade and colleague.

Fr. Lobo in his statement said, that when he noted that the said rebel priests obstinately persisted with their intent to drive out the Portuguese, he strongly felt the need to intimate *Arcebispo Primaz* and accordingly he moved to Panjim on July 31, 1787, and deposed before *Provizor e Vigario Geral* on August 5, 1787.[13]

Fr. Coutinho had initially seemed well-disposed towards Toscano but in the course of time, the conspiracy to exclude and isolate Toscano, exposed him. Fr. Lobo combined with Fr. Coutinho took a decision to make separate but simultaneous denunciations. Therefore Fr. Coutinho made his deposition at the office of *Arcebispo Primaz* on August 5, 1787.[14] It was nothing short of betrayal.

There were two other natives who strongly felt the need to denounce — Fr. Inacio Xavier Monis of Aldona and the Vicar of Socorro, Fr. Pedro José Cardozo.

Fr. Inacio Xavier Monis never did cotton to the idea of the rebellion. He first learnt of it in May 1787 at the residence of Fr. Couto in Panjim, but did not report about it as he felt it was nonsensical. But later when he went to the church of Pomburpa on one of the last days of July, perhaps on the occasion of the Feast of Santa Anna, he noticed that Fr. Lobo and Fr. Coutinho were talking secretly. He overheard them speaking about the revolt and that they should denounce the same. This spurred Fr. Monis to take a decision to make his denunciation as well.[15]

The Vicar of Soccoro, Fr. Pedro José Cardozo was from the start perturbed with the news of the impending revolt, which in his opinion was audacious. Debates were held on the matter in his Parochial House at Soccoro in June 1787. From the start he planned to report the matter to the authorities but was impeded by a grave illness. As he felt better on August 4, 1787 he made his denuciation in writing.[16]

History has been full of times, when aspirations have been fulfilled and glory achieved. It has also been full of strange behaviour of otherwise normal people, odd acts in the name of barely thought-out philosophies and happy results from unplanned actions. In the case of the nativist rebellion of 1787, it did not take off. It was nipped in the bud, was aborted and unsuccessful, squarely because of acts of betrayal.

REFERENCES

1. AHU: *MI* Maço 155(153), Devassa, undtd. Statement of Inacio Caetano Toscano.
2. AHU *MI* Maço 155(153), Devassa, undtd. Statement of Inacio Caetano Toscano.
3. AHU: *MI* Maço 155(153), Devassa, undtd. Statement of Inacio Caetano Toscano.
4. AHU: *MI* Maço 155(153), Devassa, undtd. Statement of Inacio Caetano Toscano.
5. AHU: *MI* Maço 155(153), Devassa, Auto No. 6, Statement of Inacio

Caetano Toscano.

6. AHU: *MI* Maço 155(153), Devassa, undtd. Statement of Inacio Caetano Toşcano.
7. AHU: *MI* Maço 155(153), Devassa, undtd. Statement of Inacio Caetano Toscano.
8. AHU: *MI* Maço 155(153), Devassa, undtd. Statement of Inacio Caetano Toscano.
9. AHU: *MI* Maço 155(153), Devassa, undtd. Statement of Inacio Caetano Toscano.
10. AHU: *MI* Maço 155(153), Devassa, undtd. Statement of Inacio Caetano Toscano.
11. AHU: *MI* Maco 155(153) Devassa, Denunciation of Nicolao Luis da Costa.
12. AHU: *MI* Maço 155(153), Devassa, Denunciation of Nicolao Luis da Costa.
13. AHU: *MI* Maço 155(153), Devassa, Witness No. 7, Statement of Fr. Pedro Caetano José Lobo.
14. AHU: *MI* Maço 155(153), Devassa, Auto No. 6, Statement of Inacio Caetano Toscano.
15. AHU: *MI* Maço 155(153), Devassa, Witness No. 10, Statement of Inacio Xavier Monis.
16. AHU: *MI* Maço 155(153), Devassa, Statement of Fr. Mestre Filipe de Mello.

8

BETRAYAL: THE DENUNCIATIONS

The story of the betrayal of the movement to stage a revolt in 1787 against the Portuguese, to drive them out of India, began with the denunciations made from August 5, 1787 onwards. Some natives spilt the beans to the authorities with respect to other natives, some rebels worked against other rebels. The rebels were a motley mix of the religious and the non-religious, in which the latter were in the majority, but the betrayers were mostly clerics. Apart from other reasons for the denunciations, including antipathy, the core issue was that they became alarmed that danger was closing in and feared reprisals.

One needs to point out to the role of the brother of Tenente Inacio Caetano Toscano, namely Antonio Eugenio Toscano, who on August 5, 1787, leaked the plot at the office of the Governor General, which helped to warn the authorities of the impending revolt. On the same day Coronel Manoel Godinho de Mira submitted the denunciation of Tenente Nicolao Luis da Costa of the Legion of Bardez to the authorities.[1] Costa's denunciation was placed before the Dezembargador Secretario do Estado on August 6, 1787 in the morning. An all inclusive deposition of three priests, taken under oath, was submitted to the Governor General on the same day, by the Office of *Arcebispo Primaz*.[2]

It would not be out of order, if the denunciations as submitted to the authorities, are reproduced below.

Denunciation of Tenente Nicolao Luis da Costa[3]

Nicolao Luis da Costa, 32 years of age, from the village of Parra, attached to the *Segundo Legião de Bardez* made the following deposition on August 6, 1787 which was countersigned by Sebastião José Ferreira Barroco, Dezembargador Secretario do Estado.

(1) Around 15 to 20 days ago (mid-July) while the Deponent was in his *Quartel* in the company of Inacio Caetano Toscano, Tenente of the same Legion, they recieved a message (*recado*) from Fr. José Antonio Gonsalves, who had been earlier Vicar of Chorão and was for two or three days, visiting the parish of Moira, that he desired to meet them.

(2) The Deponent, for friendship sake, along with Inacio Caetano Toscano, went to the House of the Vicar of Moira on the scheduled day. Present there was the said Vicar, Fr. Gonsalves and another priest namely Fr. Caetano da Silva, Vicar of S. Lourenço de Linhares. After dinner, the Vicar of Moira left and both the Deponent and Toscano remained behind with the two priests.

(3) Fr. José Antonio Gonsalves took him to the *alpendre* of the church. Later his comrade Toscano also came to the said *alpendre*.

(4) Fr. José Antonio Gonsalves began questioning the Deponent on the situation in the land. In this respect he referred to Tipu. The Deponent responded that he had no news of any movements relating to him. But in the next summer there was the posssibility of the Nawab

approaching Quitur. Fr. Gonsalves pondered on what would be the fate of the people of Goa, if he came to their lands. He felt that, because of the formidable and matchless forces of Tipu, the Portuguese would leave and the people would either die as martyrs for their religion or they would be converted into Muslims.

(5) The Deponent responded that the said Nawab had recently encircled Cabo de Rama. The Portuguese with a few *Sipais* had defended it well. The discipline in the forces of Goa was superior to that in the troops of Tipu. To this, the said priest said, that the Portuguese had done much wrong to the natives in the field of religion. They practiced partiality. They did not give promotions in the army and were vexatious in their system of recruitment. While they accepted that the natives were meritorious, they did not give them awards. The Deponent did not accept that the natives were maltreated. He said the troops were doing a great job. On seeing that the Deponent did not take his words seriously or that he demonstrated no interest, the priest did not spell out his intentions in clear terms. The Deponent said categorically, that the priest wanted to instigate the natives to oppose the Portuguese.

(6) The said priest requested the Deponent to incite his friends, natives and the Portuguese *casados*. In this manner he ended the conversation on that day.

(7) On returning to his *Quartel* with his comrade Inacio Caetano Toscano, the latter informed him, that the said priest José Antonio Gonsalves, had a similar conversation with him and had made the same request of getting together some friends. The Deponent concluded that the said priest had requested him to influence some Portuguese *casados*. But the priest had used a general word 'friends'.

(8) Fr. Caetano da Silva had also entered into the conversation. He spoke about what was necessary for the good of the country.

(9) Then one day, the Deponent received an intimation (*aviso*) from Fr. José Antonio Gonsalves, not to deal with the issue that was discussed with him, as Fr. Pedro, who served as Vicar of Tivim had dissuaded them.

(10) On the receipt of this *aviso*, the Deponent and his comrade proceeded to the house of Fr. Pedro. He told them that Fr. José Antonio Gonsalves and Fr. Caetano da Silva disclosed to him their intentions, because of which he dissuaded them. It was for this reason they had received the *aviso* that day. The Deponent recalled that there were two important days— that on one day, he spoke to the priests at Moira and that on the other, he spoke to Fr. Pedrinho.

(11) Fr. Pedro told the Deponent, that he tried to convince the priests not to proceed with anything that would harm anyone in the *Estado*, that it would be better that all should remain silent.

(12) The said comrade of the Deponent, on the day of Santiago, had gone to the house of Fr. Pedro and discovered that the said priests José Antonio Gonsalves and Caetano da Silva still pursued their plans. Toscano felt that they should denounce the same, so that they would not be treated as accomplices.

(13) His comrade informed all this to the Deponent and begged of him that they should both make a denunciation. The Deponent informed the matter to Coronel Manoel Godinho de Mira on August 4, 1787.

(14) The Deponent had no knowledge as to whether the said priests had persuaded other persons and neither did he

try to persuade anyone. His comrade had informed him that he had spoken about the matter to a priest in Aldona called Fr. Vicente, who reprimanded him and told him that it was best not to discuss it with anyone. Toscano had also spoken about the matter with a Cabo called Sebastião.

(15) The Deponent did not know of the steps taken by the said priests, where all they had travelled nor had he heard anything more about this matter.

In summary, the above denunciation incriminated the two priests Fr. Gonsalves and Fr. da Silva, described the happenings at Moira and Tivim specially the reaction of Fr. Pedro Caetano José Lobo and also the mind of Inacio Caetano Toscano on the matter. The two Tenentes had decided to make a joint denunciation. But Tenente Costa did it on his own, keeping Toscano in the dark, and thus betrayed his comrade.

It needs to be pointed out at this stage that despite the above discussed denunciation, Tenente Costa did not escape the label of an accomplice. While on trial, he was found guilty by the authorities and was one of the fifteen sent to the gallows.

Depositions were made by three priests—Fr. Inacio Xavier Monis, Fr. Vicente Filipe Coutinho and Fr. Pedro Caetano José Lobo before *Provizor e Vigario Geral* Antonio Silveira de Menezes and Fr. Antonio Gomes, *Escrivão* for the purpose. The priests intimated the *Arcebispo Primaz* about how Fr. José Antonio Gonsalves, Fr. Caetano Francisco de Couto and Fr. Caetano da Silva joined hands with others and had attempted to conspire against the *Estado da India.* Fr. Menezes forwarding the depositions, informed the civil authorities that the rebels were also composed of native military officers and soldiers. They had influenced the bakers to introduce poison in the bread to end the lives of those necessary for the defence of the State. It appeared that the conspirators had even instigated enemy countries to help in the rebellion. The Vicars had spread the information about the proposed rebellion, from parish to parish, in the *Arcebispado*. Fr. Menezes held that exemplary punishment should be imposed on the conspirators for which trial proceedings should be initiated.[4]

Denunciation of Fr. Inacio Xavier Monis[5]

Fr. Inacio Xavier Monis, 32 years of age, native of the village of Aldona, of the Province of Bardez, under oath submitted the following testimony.

Fr. Monis said at about 10 o'clock in the morning of May 18, 1787 he was a witness to the happenings in the residence of Fr. Caetano Francisco de Couto at Panjim. There he met Fr. José Felipe Gonsalves, a native of Piedade, who had in his company an official of the Legion, a native, but he was ignorant of his name. There was also a soldier whose name was perhaps Salvador da Costa. They were in conversation in the hall. The said priest José Filipe Gonsalves then rose and took him (Fr. Monis) to an inner room where they were joined by Fr. Caetano Francisco de Couto. Fr. Gonsalves began his talk saying "We have succeeded in getting several persons not only in the Province of Salcette and Bardez but also from Ilhas, for expelling the Portuguese from this Capital". He told Fr. Monis to be on the look out for persons who would agree to do their bit to take forward their plans, that this should be treated as an inviolable secret. To this, he (Fr. Monis) responded that he was a poor man and that he would not be able to cooperate with the project. Fr. José Filipe caught hold of him and told him that the natives would be bestowed with honours and pre-eminences. If he could not help, he could at least do it through others in the village of Aldona. He recalled that in that village there were influential people there like Fr. Vicente Filipe Coutinho and Damião Mathias. Fr. Monis responded that he did not have a brother or a relative, who could be of use and that none of them were interested in pre-eminences. With these words he bid them goodbye. He told them that it was time for dinner and returned back to the house of Fr. Luis Caetano de Souza, where he was a guest.

Fr. Monis was about to depart from the house of the said Fr. Luis Caetano de Souza, his relative in the town of Panjim, when he received a message, an unsigned chit from Fr. Francisco Caetano de Couto, that he (Fr. Monis) should meet him. He sent this *chito* with a boy who had handed it to Fr. Luis Caetano de Souza. On reading it Fr. Monis proceeded to the residence of the said priest (Fr. Couto) which was in the neighbourhood. On meeting the said Fr. Couto, he was taken to the same inner room where earlier Fr. José Filipe had spoken to him. This time too Fr. José Filipe was present. Both of them accused the witness of having deceived them the last time when they had discussed about the rebellion. They insisted that he should at least now keep it secret.

On hearing this the witness responded that he did not wish to be involved in such matters and that he was a poor young man not interested in honours and grandeur. For which Fr. José Filipe said "It is alright son, but guard the secret and not disclose anything to anyone". These were the details that Fr. Monis had deposed relating to Fr. Caetano Francisco de Couto and Fr. José Antonio Gonsalves.

Denunciation of Fr. Vicente Filipe Coutinho.[6]

Fr. Vicente Filipe Coutinho, 37 years of age, was a native of Aldona. He promised to divulge all that happened when questioned.

Fr. Coutinho informed that on a day in July, 1787 at 2o'clock in the afternoon, there appeared at his house Fr. José Vas, a native of Anjuna, of the province of Bardez, along with a secular person Inacio Toscano, a native of Aldona, Tenente of the new Legion of Bardez. As Fr. José Vas did not have any acquaintance with the Deponent, the Tenente called upon him and informed him of a *sublevação* (revolt) planned by the natives of this Capital to expel the whites. Fr. Coutinho questioned about this diabolic plan and as to how this could be accomplished. To this the Tenente replied that Fr. José Vas did not know Fr. Coutinho, that he had requested the Tenente to introduce him in his house, in order to have an opportunity to speak to him about the matter.

The said Tenente informed Fr. Coutinho that Fr. José Vas had promised money about 4000 *xerafins* to entice the native soldiers in his Legion to participate in the revolt. For the same goal, the matter was discussed with several natives—ecclesiastic and secular. One of them had influenced the bakers to introduce poison in the bread on the day fixed for the revolt, in order to end all the whites. They also had a recipe for a drink by which the soldiers for a period of five days would be unconscious. In Cuncolim, 1000 men were arranged. Likewise persons were arranged in various parts of the Province of Bardez, in Sivolim and in other districts of the same Province. Fr. Coutinho decided not to get involved in the matter that the priest Fr. Vas had proposed.

At 7 o'clock on another night in July, 1787. Fr. José Antonio Gonsalves, native of Piedade and Fr. Caetano da Silva, Vicar of São Lourenço de Linhares, met the brother of Fr. Coutinho namely Paulo Benedicto Coutinho on the *prayas de Volotim*, district of the parish of Pomburpa. Both the priests greeted the said Paulo Benedicto, and asked him if his brother (Fr. Vicente) was available. He replied that perhaps he was not there. Fr. Vicar stated that they had come for a *dependencia* but Fr. Gonsalves did not divulge anything and remained reserved. They had come in search of Fr. Vicente Coutinho at his house. They bid goodbye to Paulo Benedicto and left him puzzled. The latter returned to his house where Fr. Vicente Filipe Coutinho also lived. The latter gave an account of all that had happened to him and said that the *dependencia* was nothing else but that which was proposed by Fr. José Vas, who was not able to discuss the issue with him on his own, but spoke to him through Tenente Toscano.

He learnt that the said priests José Antonio Gonsalves and Caetano da Silva were for three days in the Parochial House of the church of Moira, where two native officials of the New Legion of Bardez were called. They spent the night there. From there the said priests moved to the church of Tivim in the said month of July, a little before the feast of St. Christopher and conducted the same conversation with the Vicar of the said parish, Fr. Pedro Caetano José Lobo, who did not give much importance to the matter.

Tenente Toscano gave the impression that at the appropriate occasion, help would be given by Germany, whose natives were residing in the Capital, and that they would participate in the revolt, that in this *Corte* one could use a German engineer for the said end.

Fr. Coutinho stated that in the Parochial House of the church of Pilerne there was a stranger brought by Fr. José Antonio. The latter had disembarked at Cochin while on the return voyage from Portugal to India. He had also travelled alone to the southern coast.

He now recalled that it was on July 4, that Fr. José Vas had come in search of him at his home.

Denunciation of Fr. Pedro Caetano José Lobo.[7]

Fr. Pedro Caetano José Lobo, native of Pomburpa, about 40 years of age, Vicar of the church of St. Christopher of Tivim, under oath, promised to speak the truth about what he knew and when questioned.

Fr. Lobo said that on July 17 or 18, at the church of Tivim which was under his control, there appeared at about two o'clock in the afternoon, the Vicar of São Lourenço de Linhares, Caetano da Silva, native of Sirula and Fr. José Antonio Gonsalves, native of Piedade. They had come from the church of Moira, where they had stayed for three days. After the intitial greetings the Vicar of São Lourenço de Linhares expressed a wish to speak to Fr. Lobo confidentially. They therefore moved to an inner room of the Parochial House. The Vicar (Fr. da Silva) in a loud voice stated that the natives of the *Estado da India* had suffered much under the whites and that Her Majesty, the Queen had taken a stand of not listening to this *Corte*. The same was reiterated by his companion Fr. José Antonio Gonsalves. He said that the natives were not allowed to occupy public posts and receive honours. They were told by Fr. Caetano Vitorino de Faria, who was at Lisbon, that the natives should raise the banner of revolt. They had succeeded in arousing many natives, mainly of the Provinces of Salcette and Ilhas, who had joined the movement. They had many men of arms in Cuncolim. This was arranged through the intervention of Bastião de Noronha, a merchant of Salcette and now Assistant in Panjim. With the help of the said person and Fr. Caetano Francisco de Couto, native of Panjim, they would work to conquer the courage of the natives living in Panjim, to end the lives of the military of the *Companhia da Guarda* of His Excellency the Governor General and the whites in the *Artilharia*. For this end they had the support of many people. They had enough money to carry out a thorough and complete revolt. The natives of Bardez had also entered into this plot. The Legion was expected to agree to this through the efforts of its officials Inacio Toscano and Nicolao Luis da Costa, Tenentes of the Legion and natives of this country. The Legion of Ponda was already influenced by Tenente Manoel Caetano Pinto, native of Candolim. The said Fr. José Antonio Gonsalves had got hold of Narba Naique. The former asked Fr.

Lobo, whether as a principal citizen of the village of Pomburpa and Sirula, he would agree to support the proposed rebellion and arrange an agent and obtain from Assonora and other parts, at least 100 Muslims, to be kept hidden in the church of Pomburpa. In case money was required for this *dependencia* it would be promptly given.

On hearing all this, Fr. Lobo was quite puzzled. As he appeared confused, the said Vicar (Fr. da Silva) turned to his companion and said "Let us declare everything to this priest". To this, the said Fr. José Antonio responded positively. He began saying that involved in the revolt were many natives, both secular and ecclesiastic. They were Vicars of the parishes of Pilerne, Pomburpa, two *Congregado Padres* Sebastião Baptista and Pedro Dalgado and Fr. João Baptista Pinto, brother of Tenente Manoel Caetano Pinto. To all this, Fr. Lobo listened with much dismay and sorrow . His Curate Fr. Baltazar Rodrigues who had entered the room felt the same way. The said Vicar and Fr. José Antonio Gonsalves did not go to the house of Fr. Vicente Coutinho of Aldona where they were supposed to go for the same purpose. Fr. Lobo learnt that Fr. Vicente Coutinho did not agree with the proposal. He did not want to be involved and remained reserved. They also informed in writing to Tenentes Inacio Toscano and Nicolao Luis da Costa not to undertake the work they were told to do.

Consequently, both the Tenentes came to speak to Fr. Lobo. He gave them a tongue lashing in the presence of his Curate and the *Escrivão* of the village of Tivim, Tomas Antonio Pereira. The said officers on listening to him raised their hands to the heavens saying "Thank God they were free of the harrasment of the said priests", that they had not spoken to the soldiers of their Legion in the manner in which the priests desired.

Further he said that, on the next day the priests left the Parochial House of Tivim. Fr. Lobo bid good bye to the priests who said that they would be going home. But on the contrary they went to the church of Pomburpa, whose Vicar was the brother of the Vicar of Pilerne and the latter was the brother - in - law of Fr. José Antonio Gonsalves. They remained there for some days. From there they proceeded to the house of the Vicar of Reys Magos in Sirula, where they stopped for a few days. In this house were the said Vicar of Reys Magos, Antonio Caetano Lobo and his nephews Avelino Lourenço Lobo and José Caetano Lobo. Fr. José Antonio had told them that he had engineers in the capital to mine the area. A special drink was being prepared by which the soldiers for some days would be unconscious.

He heard that in the church of Pilerne, a foreigner was seen, who was taken there by Fr. José Antonio. He had come from the South. Fr. Lobo also heard that in the said church of Pilerne, the priests would meet for the said *sublevação*. He said further that the said Fr. José Antonio Gonsalves told him (Fr. Lobo) that on the day fixed for the revolt, the bakers would introduce poison in the bread and end the lives of the whites. Moreover he said that Fr. José Ribeiro, who was presently in the service of the Marathas at Pune, was consulted in the matter of the proposed revolt. He was asked to arrange some men and send them to this *Corte* when intimated.

Fr. Lobo further stated that on the fixed day the rebels would make the forces of the Regiment at Rachol march. They had prepared rubrics of the Governor General in order to issue the necessary orders.

Denunciation made by Fr. Pedro José Cardozo.[8]

Fr. Pedro José Cardozo, Vicar of the Church of Soccoro, wanted to denounce the conspiracy earlier but was unwell. He first made his declaration on July 31, 1787 which reached the concerned authorities on August 4. When he was better he sent a written statement addressed to Sebastião José Ferreira Barroco, which the latter received on August 9, at 8.30 in the morning.

Fr. Cardozo stated that as he was critically ill, on bed, for almost three months, he could not intimate the following earlier.

On June 8, there suddenly arrived at the church of Socorro, Fr. José Antonio Gonsalves, a native of Piedade and Fr. João Baptista Pinto, a native of Candolim, persons with whom he did not have much relationship. They were just acquaintances, whom he had met, while studying in the *Colegio de Chorão* and at other places. They wanted to entertain themselves having baths at his house for some days. He could not deny them this, because of his past acquaintance with them. Perhaps, four or five days later, came Fr. Caetano Francisco de Couto, a native of Panjim. They got together and began to engage themselves in discussions. He heard them protesting about the oppressed state of the natives in Goa and of the country. They proposed its improvement and advanced various ideas. They said that some of these they could not accomplish, without offence to the rule of Her Majesty. It seemed to him that some of the ideas were seditious and he therefore argued with them about it. He also questioned the vanity and temerity with which they were discussing such matters. There was no nod from his side. In fact he pointed out that the project they were planning was senseless, and that he was not willing to be a part of it. In fact all this disgusted him a lot.

They moved out of his house after eight days. They left him in such disturbed spirits, that this worsened his illness, that is a urinary problem combined with strong continental fevers. On June 16, he immediately moved from the church of Socorro to his house, situated in the parish of Salvador do Mundo in the same village, where he remained because of the gravity of his illness. It went on worsening with the development of various complications and he feared that the end was near. He called for Fr. Filipe do Melo for a general confession and expressed his anxiety about all that he had learnt, all that was spoken to him, all that was proposed and the seditious spirit of the rebels. The said priest said that he knew them well and that he (Fr. Cardozo) should report everything to *Arcebispo Primaz* and free himself of his obligations. Taking into consideration his bad condition, the priest offered to do it for him. This was perhaps on July 31. It was received by the authorities on August 4. He did not know on which day it was done, as he was sick. He was now bed-ridden and in a terrible state. He has now respectfully submitted this report in writing, though it was compulsory on his part to meet the authorities personally. Fr. Cardozo revealed all the caprices and ideas that he heard from the said persons in great detail and with all the truth at his disposal.

Meanwhile Fr. Cardozo passed away and his brother Salvador Francisco Cardozo gave a statement on August 25, 1787. He stated that, he was the brother of the deceased Fr. Pedro José Cardozo, who had been Vicar of Socorro. Salvador had written the above-mentioned letter, which was as dictated by his dying brother.

All the denunciations made above bear testimony to the proposed rebellion of 1787 and also paint a picture of downright treachery and betrayal.

REFERENCES

1. HAG: *MR* 169A, fl. 197.
2. AHU: *MI* Maço 155(153), doc. dtd. 19 Aug. 1787.
3. AHU: *MI* Maço 155(153), Denunciation of Nicolao Luis da Costa.
4. AHU: *MI* Maço 155(153), Letter of Fr. Antonio Silveira de Menezes.
5. AHU: *MI* Maço 155(153), Denunciation of Fr. Inacio Xavier Monis.
6. AHU: *MI* Maço 155(153), Denunciation of Fr. Vicente Filipe Coutinho.
7. AHU: *MI* Maço 155(153), Denunciation of Fr. Pedro Caetano José Lobo.
8. AHU: *MI* Maço 155(153), Denunciation of Fr. Pedro José Cardozo, doc. dtd. 8 August 1787.

9

OFFICIAL REACTION AND RESPONSE : IMMEDIATE STEPS TAKEN

From August 6, 1787 to August 9, 1787 : Arrests and Security Measures

Denunciations made on August 5 and August 6, 1787 disclosed the outbreak of an intended nativist rebellion. Reprisals were bound to follow.

Fearing that any delay may cause violence and chaos, the authorities immediately rushed into action. Orders were issued on August 6, for the arrests of all those suspected to be responsible. Not only were arrests made promptly, but also the papers and documents found in the possession of the rebels, seized.[1] Another order was released on August 9, for punitive action—proceedings to be initiated against the accused for a Devassa (trial).[2]

Anticipating danger, steps were also taken to enquire into whether there was any involvement of an enemy power. The authorities felt, that the matter was quite grave, that it had taken the form of a rebellion, which could have involved some sudden and unforeseen movement. There was no certainty, that the rebels had not communicated with any of the neighbouring rulers.

A matter of concern for the authorities was the internal unity of the *Estado* as well as its security and protection, as around were powerful enemies, mainly the Nawab Tipu Sultan. Although the *Estado* was ready with arms, yet it was possible for powerful enemies to take advantage of an internal dissention. Therefore care was taken, that what had transpired in Goa, did not spread beyond the inevitable and that the neighbouring rulers should treat the issue as a matter of little importance. It was not only felt prudent by the Goa authorities but they also had reservations, about sending a complete report to Portugal by the *Não Conceição* which had reached Goa on September 12, 1787.[3]

On August 7, at the break of dawn in one swoop Fr. Caetano Francisco de Couto, some Vicars and priests, four Tenentes and many non-religious persons were arrested.[4] Although most of the rebels were arrested, a few escaped. Four priests managed to flee, one of them was Fr. José Antonio Gonsalves, who was the most active, shrewd and the true leader of the aborted rebellion. He had fled to the lands of the Marathas.[5] The others who managed to escape were Fr. José Manoel Ribeiro, Fr. Diego Caetano de Couto and Fr. Pedro Fernandes of Assagão.[6] Fr. Inacio de Noronha and his brothers Xavier dos Remedios Noronha and Josepha fled to Bombay.

The following is a *Relação* (List) of those who were arrested upto August 9, 1787:-[7]

In the Aguada Fort

1. Tenente of Legion of Ponda, Manoel Caetano Pinto
2. Tenente of the same Legion, Pedro Luis Gonzaga de Souza
3. Tenente of the Legion of Bardez, Nicolao Luis da Costa.
4. Tenente of the same Legion, Inacio Caetano Toscano.
5. Fr. Caetano Francisco de Couto
6. Fr. Luis Caetano de Souza
7. Vicar of Pomburpa, Fr. João Alvares de Souza

8. Geraldo Ferreira, native of Arpora
9. Salvador da Costa, native of Parra
10. Sardessai Narba Naique
11. Sebastião Barboza, cook of the Vicar of Pilerne
12. Domingos de Souza attached to the Vicar of Pilerne.

In the Fort of Reys Magos

1. Vicar of S. Lourenço de Linhares, Fr. Caetano da Silva
2. Vicar of Pilerne, Fr. Miguel Alvares
3. Fr. Vicente Alvares, brother of Vicar of Pilerne
4. Fr. José Vas, resident of Anjuna
5. Vicar of Moira
6. Fr. João Baptista Pinto

In the Quartel of Pangim

1. Manoel Francisco Gonsalves, resident of Piedade
2. Fr. Luis Antonio Gonsalves, resident of Piedade

From the above it is clear that the arrested were housed at three sites, namely Fort Aguada, Fort of Reys Magos and the *Quartel* in Panjim. The authorities in Goa were compelled to employ European troops for guarding the above said prisoners , perhaps, because native forces could not be relied on. This created a lack of forces for the security of the State. Therefore Portugal was asked to dispatch more European troops.[8]

The developments in Goa from August 5 to 9, 1787 were reported in detail in letters addressed to Martinho de Melo e Castro, Secretario do Estado da India. They were sent through Bombay.[9]

Steps taken in Salcette : Arrest of Sebastião de Noronha

On August 11, 1787 Tristão Vas da Veiga Cabral attached to the *Palacio de Pangim*, submitted the following report on the measures he had taken in the province of Salcette.[10]

On August 7, Senhor Marechal received the first order from the Governor. Consequently, he dispatched the Sargento of the *Premiera Companhia* of the *Premeiro Regimento* with two soldiers in disguise, to arrest Sebastião de Noronha at Nagoa. But the latter had fled. He had climbed a hill next to his house.

Viega Cabral then sent Senhor Marechal who moved from the Praça de Rachol on August 8, at 9 o'clock in the night, directly to Nagoa . Within two or three quarters of an hour he had encircled the house of Noronha, with 30 persons. In the said house was a priest, named Nicolao Manoel Rebello, a native of Chicalim whom they detained and José Matias de Silveira of the Island of S. Matias, who said that he was there to prepare an *escritura.* This person along with Pascoal dos Remedios, neighbour of Noronha were arrested and later brought to Rachol. But before this, as soon as it dawned, in the presence of the said priest and other persons, the wife of the fugitive, was made to open boxes, brief cases and a small *bau de pão*. From this, the elements of distrust were obvious. There was not more than a *rupia* in the house, nor was there gold and silver or anything of value. Eventually, Maria Florinda, wife of Noronha was also moved to Rachol and was handed over to Cabo Pouvação.

In Cuncolim, there were no persons seen outside the *Condado* nor any suspicious behaviour from the public.

T. da Costa, brother of the Cabo of the Legion said that Noronha had an important agent in Assolna, who came from the South, named João Onorcar, who was arrested on August 10, and was kept in the *Tronco de Rachol*.

By an order dated August 11, 1787 issued by Marechal de Campo Viega, the Cabo of the village of Nagoa was instructed to render and execute all the help that was required by Caetano Xavier da Costa, Cabo da Esquadra of the Legion, who was entrusted with a duty of *Real Serviço* of the Her Majesty.[11] A similar order was issued to the Cabos of the villages of the Province of Salcette, where the Cabo da Esquadra would proceed for the execution of the same duty.[12]

Costa carried out his duty as per the order issued to him by the said Marechal. After locating the place where Noronha was in hiding, the latter was arrested. To help in these operations, he used the services of a *cafre* who had met the brother of Noronha. Later some persons attacked José Cafre. They cracked his head showing their anger and vengeance for the work done by him.[13] They were however arrested. The events leading to their arrest can be traced from the statement made by José Cafre during the trial.

José Cafre had been called by the *Escrivão* of the village of Nagoa to cook for a function i.e. the birthday of his daughter. It was planned to celebrate the day with a grand dinner. There was a huge gathering for the function, and the people were enjoying themselves with food and drink. A group of them, began behaving in a disorderly manner. José requested them not to misbehave. This group included Caetano Velho, Lourenço Castello, Paulo Dias and Xavier Dias of the same village. Late that night José decided to leave the house of the *Escrivão*. At the door of the said house, Lourenço Castello and Caetano Velho seized him and hit him on the head with a bamboo stick. José was showered with the words, "You have arrested Sebastião de Noronha". José responded "I have not arrested him. He was arrested at the orders of His Excellency". The four persons were not relatives of Sebastião de Noronha nor were they well-acquainted with him. The wives of Lourenço Castello and Caetano Velho approached José, pleading with him, not to complain and even offered him two *santomes*. But because of his complaint, arrest orders were issued and Lourenço Castello and Caetano Velho were arrested.[14]

Seizure of Letters from the *Nau de Viagem*

From the ship that came from Portugal in the monsoon of 1787, some letters were seized by the authorities. The first letter was from José Antonio of the family of the Pintos of Candolim addressed to his brother Fr. João Baptista Pinto, one of the main rebels of the revolt.[15] The second was written by a young man called Joaquim Antonio and the remaining two letters were written by Eloy José Correa Peixoto.[16] The last three above-mentioned letters, were all addressed to Fr. José Antonio Gonsalves, one of the ringleaders and in fact the true leader of the proposed rebellion.

The letters throw light on the minds of those based in Lisbon with respect to Goa and its natives. Of significance was their connection with the rebels, Fr. José Antonio Gonsalves and João Baptista Pinto. For instance, the two letters written by Eloy José Correa Peixoto show his deep respect and veneration for Fr. Gonsalves. They also revealed a great deal of anxiety as to whether Fr. Gonsalves had reached India safely. The last time Peixoto had heard about Fr. Gonsalves was in February 1786, when the *Nau de Viagem* left Lisbon. Peixoto also sent his regards to Fr. Caetano Francisco de Couto, another ringleader of the revolt.[17]

In the letter of José Antonio Pinto to his brother Fr. João Baptista Pinto there were pointed references to their brother Tenente Manoel Caetano Pinto of the Legion of Ponda, who was due for a *patente* of *Capitão de Infantaria*. He clearly tells his brother Fr. Pinto that Tenente Manoel should not wait for *Patentes Superiores,* that they were given only to *reinois*. Moreover, they were conferred on less meritorious persons, even *degredados*.[18]

José Antonio Pinto further writes about the ways for the future happiness of Goa, that no one knew well as they (those based in Lisbon), what was Goa and what was Europe.[19]

The letter written by Joaquim to Fr. Gonsalves states that he was engulfed in misfortunes. He wrote about his interview with Martinho de Melo Castro, that he had submitted attestations of Dr. Faria, Dr. Ciera and Dr. Brunely and the testimonials spoke glowingly of his intelligence, talent and character. [20] It must be said that few had completed the course of *Marinha* at the *Academia.* Joaquim in fact had distinguished himself as one of the best *finalistas* of the *Academia.*[21] Joaquim commented that he wished to return to his unfortunate motherland in the monsoon of 1787.

Investigations in the Legion of Ponda

When the news of the arrests of the rebels broke out, there were denunciations made from within the ranks of the army. The first to do it was Fr. Francisco José de Jesus Maria, Chaplain of the Legion of Ponda and Cabo Manoel Ferrão on August 8. This was followed by another denunciation made by Cabo Antonio Fernandes of the Companhia No.10 on August 9. These denunciations reported on the role of Tenente Gonzaga, Tenente Pinto, already behind bars, as well as others in the Legion of Ponda for their involvement in the intended revolt. The denunciations were made before their military superiors. They are reproduced and examined below.

Denunciation made by Fr. Francisco José de Jesus Maria.[22]

On August 8, Fr. Francisco José de Jesus Maria, made a denunciation against Francisco Pereira. *Ajudante de Cirurgia* of the Legion of Ponda stating that on August 6, the said *Ajudante de Cirurgia* had come to him at 11.30 in the morning. The latter told him that he had a secret to tell him and therefore they moved to a room. He appeared confused and sought the priest's advice. He told him that Tenente Gonzaga had informed him of a plot against the Portuguese to be staged between August 20 and August 24. The priest advised the said *Ajudante de Cirurgia* to report it to the Brigadier. The said *Ajudante de Cirurgia* responded that it would be better first to speak to the *Marechal* and then proceed to the *Brigadeiro*. Fr. Jesus Maria asked him, whether it was possible for them (natives) to govern. The said *Ajudante de Cirurgia* responded that they would be governors (rulers) and that justice would be administered properly. This was what the said Tenente Gonzaga told him. The *Ajudante de Cirurgia* however felt remorse of conscience, as this was an action intended against Her Majesty, the Queen. He therefore came to the priest to seek his advice as to before whom he should make his denunciation. As it was a matter to be given considerable thought, Fr. Jesus Maria told the *Ajudante* that they would meet in the evening to decide as to the future steps to be taken.

As the *Ajudante* was busy with his duties of attending to the sick, as part of his work in *Administração dos Remedios*, he could not meet the said priest that evening. Fr. Jesus Maria was not a Brahmin, nor a Gauncar nor was the said *Ajudante de Cirurgia*. Therefore to safeguard their future, the priest took a decision that in the morning on the following day on August 7, he would report to the *Brigadeiro*. But on the same morning arrests were made.

On August 8, in the evening Fr. Jesus Maria reported to the authorities the entire conversation he had with the *Ajudante de Cirurgia*. Fr. Jesus Maria's denunciation implicated not only Tenente Gonzaga but also the *Ajudante de Cirurgia*. He categorically stated he had no direct interaction with Tenente Gonzaga about the proposed revolt.

In response to the denunciation of Fr. Jesus Maria, Francisco Pereira, *Ajudante de Cirurgia* confirmed much that had been expressed by the priest. He said further that Tenente Gonzaga had first told him (the *Ajudante*), that the Vicar of the parish of Ponda Fr. Manoel da Expectação had already joined the movement for the said rebellion and that on the next day a message was sent to him telling him not to do anything, as matters were not good. These words caused discomfort in the said Vicar.[23]

Denunciation made by Cabo Antonio Fernandes.[24]

Cabo Antonio Fernandes stated that about twelve days ago, he was called outside the *Guarda* by *Cirurgião mor* David Francisco Viegas. He was taken to a place where no one could hear what was being spoken. The said *Cirurgião mor* stated that soon the entire land (of Goa) would be theirs (of the natives). It would not be governed by the Portuguese. They (the natives) would have peace and things would be better. Viegas further said that it was not for now and it would be later. He spoke softly "Not now, everything was done, there is a shortage of four *companhias*, but these are not required, not to talk about it to anyone" and he left.

Viegas had emphasized the capabilities of Cabo Fernandes to convince the soldiers under him to join the same revolt and that the other *Cabos* did not have this ability. But he was also told that there was time still, and not to take it up at this stage.

The Deponent, Cabo Fernandes was asked by the authorities as to why he had not made his denunciation earlier. He replied that he thought that the matter was just a game and it would not succeed. Three days after the conversation, Cabo Fernandes had with the *Cirurgião mor* he received a message from the latter, through *Ajudante de Cirurgia,* Marcelino de Noronha that he should not disclose whatever had been discussed with anyone. The Cabo further stated that the *Ajudante de Cirurgia* (Noronha) was totally in the dark relating to the contents of the message.

Cabo Manoel Ferrão had made a denunciation against the following:-

1) Sargento Baltazar Caeiro

2) Sargento Sebastião Simões

3) Sargento José Gracias

4) Furriel Antonio Pedro

5) Furriel Joaquim Barretto

6) Furriel Pedro da Roza

7) Cabo Miguel Gaunço

8) Cabo Vitorino Simões

9) Cabo Avelino Antonio

10) Cabo Manoel Pereira

11) Cabo Pascoal Antonio

12) Cabo Sebastião Dias

13) Soldado João Vas

14) Soldado Antonio Rodrigues

15) Soldado Manoel de Aguiar

16) Soldado Xavier Dias

17) Soldado Fabião Alvares

Manoel Ferrão in his denunciation stated that Tenente Gonzaga told him that he had invited all the native officers of the Legion of Ponda. All of them were ready to be part of said conspiracy except *Sargento* and *Furriel* of *Primeira Companhia*, *Furriel* of *Terceira Companhia*, *Sargento* of *Quinta Companhia*, and the *Furriel* of *Decima Quinta Companhia*.

Accordingly Capitão José Antunes Branco reacted immediately on August 10 and 11, 1787. He acquired a statement from Cabo Manoel Ferrão and began the cross examination of all those denounced by the latter.

Deposition of Cabo Manoel Ferrão[25]

Cabo Manoel Ferrão of the *Companhia de Freitas* of which Pedro Luis Gonzaga was a Tenente, was questioned on August 11, 1787 with respect to what he declared in writing on August 8. He was asked, whether he was aware of the revolt, that the Brahmins planned to carry out against the Portuguese. He replied that when he had gone to Paroda he met Tenente Gonzaga. The latter told him that almost the whole of Bardez, Ilhas and Salcette were in a state of readiness, that all the rich native rebels were ready to kill all the Portuguese. Cabo Ferrão questioned him "Why they were not killed when they first entered these lands?". To this the said Tenente responded that in those days they were not capable of doing so. The Deponent replied that this could not be so. To this, the Tenente said "Go away". Eight days later, Cabo Ferrão was called to the *Quartel* of Tenente Gonzaga. He ordered Ferrão to sit and he stated "You do not wish to believe whatever I have told you. I shall now take an oath not to disclose to anyone whatever had been discussed between us, and you too take one". The Tenente brought out some *contas* and raised his hands above them and said that he was taking a pledge not to reveal anything, and that he should do the same. He began to repeat all that he had said earlier. To this he added the matter of arranging six legions. He said that everything was in conformity with carrying out the said revolt. Everyone was ready, including the Legion of Bardez and the Legion of Ponda. He said that he had spoken to all the rich natives of Bardez, Salcette and Ilhas, but did not disclose their names. He affirmed that they had a sufficient supply of ammunition, armament and money.

Cabo Ferrão ended his deposition stating that he knew with certainty, that Sargento Baltazar Caeiro was on Sunday, August 5, in the *Quartel* of the said Tenente Pedro Luis Gonzaga with Tenente Manoel Caetano Pinto, to deal with the business of the conspiracy. The Deponent knew this as he was present and he heard and saw everything. On the same day Tenente Gonzaga promised to make him *Alferes*.

Cabo Ferrão further declared that he was questioned by the said Tenente Gonzaga, relating to matters when he was in the Fort of Santiago as to how many Portuguese and *sipais* were stationed there, the gunpowder and *bala* available in the fort etc. To this the Deponent replied that he did not know with certainty. The Tenente made enquiries as to whether there was any passage by which one could enter and attack the fort, once the doors were closed. The Deponent responded that he had no knowledge of this, more so as it was not in his village. The Tenente further said that first they would kill the Portuguese there and then recover all that was necessary for the land.

Capitão Branco while acquiring the statements from all the military personnel denounced by Cabo Ferrão, questioned them as to whether they were invited to join the conspiracy, who had invited them and whether they were asked to persuade others.

Furriel Antonio Periera

Furriel Pereira in his statement said that Tenente Pedro Luis Gonzaga told him that some people of Bardez were planning to revolt against the Portuguese for the bad they had done. Pereira immediately interrupted him and told him that he did not want to get involved and quickly moved away. The Tenente tried to stop him but he left. He did not tell anyone about this incident which took place about 15 to 20 days back.[26]

Sargento Simões

Sargento Simões at first stated that he was a faithful servant of His Majesty for the last 21 years. He had not the slightest knowledge of the intended revolt. When confronted with the deposition of Cabo Manoel Ferrão, that stated that Tenente

Gonzaga had told Ferrão, that Sargento Simões had been invited to join the comspiracy, he denied this totally.[27]

Furriel Joaquim Baretto

In like manner Furriel Baretto indicated that he was totally ignorant about the conspiracy. He was confronted with the deposition of Manoel Ferrão, that he (Ferrão) was told by Tenente Gonzaga, that Barretto had been invited to join it and he had accepted the invitation. To this he responded that this was a lie, that not only the Tenente had not spoken to him, but that the relations between them were strained.[28]

Cabo Miguel Gaunço

Similar to the above-mentioned too instances was that of Cabo Miguel Gaunço. He too denied any involvement in the revolt and stated that he did not know Cabo Ferrão and had heard through others that he was a *Cabo de Major*.[29]

Sargento José Gracias

Sargento José Gracias too stated that he did not know about the conspiracy. He had only exchanged courtesies with Tenente Manoel Caetano Pinto. As for Tenente Gonzaga, he expressed, that he had differences with him for years. When confronted with the deposition of Cabo Manoel Ferrão, that Tenente Gonzaga had told him (Ferrão) that Gracias had been persuaded to join the conspiracy and that he showed willingness. This was denied by Gracias.[30]

Furriel Pedro da Roza

Furriel Pedro da Roza on being questioned about his involvement in the conspiracy, stated that no one had approached him relating to the same and that he had no indication of it. He was told that Manoel Ferrão had implicated him in the plot. Pedro da Roza denied the same.[31]

Cabo Vitorino Simões

Likewise Cabo Vitorino Simões in his statement denied having any discussion with Tenente Gonzaga as indicated by Manoel Ferrão. He very categorically said that the statement of Ferrão was false and that he had been ill and when slightly better he had proceeded on leave for ten days. He had not seen or met Tenente Gonzaga and Tenente Pinto.[32]

Cabo Avelino Antonio Soares

Cabo Avelino Antonio Soares in his statement expressed that he had faithfully served the Portuguese as they fed him and therefore was not part of the conspiracy. When faced with the deposition of Ferrão he very firmly indicated that it was a lie.[33]

Cabo Manoel Pereira da Cruz

On questioning Cabo Manoel Pereira da Cruz of the *Companhia de Menezes* as to his involvement in the consipiracy, he clearly stated that he was the son of a Portuguese *Capitão*. Honestorio (?) Pereira da Cruz, and that like him, was a faithful servant of Her Majesty. Relating to the statement made by Tenente Gonzaga to the Cabo Manoel Ferrão he said that he was free to say as he wished, that this was false.[34]

Cabo Pascoal Antonio

Cabo Pascoal Antonio stated that he had no knowledge of the conspiracy nor had any of the Tenentes spoken to him about it. When confronted with the deposition of Manoel Ferrão that he was party to the said revolt, he denied this totally.[35]

Soldado João Vas

João Vas, Soldado belonged to *Companhia de Freitas* of which Pedro Luis Gonzaga was the Tenente. When questioned as to whether he was invited to join the revolt against the Portuguese, who had invited him, and whether he was entrusted with the work of persuading others to join the same, he stated that he was called by Tenente Pedro Luis Gonzaga about eight days ago and the latter had explained to him that matters would be better, if they were rulers of the land, for which they would have to throw out the Portuguese. The Tenente also mentioned, that in this regard they would get the help of the Bhonsles.

João Vas further stated that on another day before this discussion he had with the Tenente, he had accompanied the said Tenente to Mandur for the feast. There he saw a gathering of almost twenty-five persons, all of whom, were Brahmins.[36]

With reference to the denunciation of Cabo Manoel Ferrão, he mentioned that the latter told him that Tenente Gonzaga had spoken to him about the proposed rebellion. He (Vas) advised him to put it down in writing. Vas was asked as to why it should be in writing. He stated that this was needed to submit to the *Brigadeiro*. When confronted with this, Cabo Ferrão did not deny this.[37]

Soldado Antonio Rodrigues

On being questioned about his involvement in the nativist plot to overthrow the Portuguese rule in Goa, Soldado Antonio Rodrigues of the *Companhia de Freitas* said that at the door of his accommodation, Soldado João Vas told him that one night they would kill the entire Legion. The Deponent asked him how this could be possible. He recalled that he (Vas) said that this would happen within four days. After this the two Tenentes Gonzaga and Pinto were arrested. When this happened, the Deponent asked João Vas, whether it was this, that he was referring to. Cabo Ferrão when confronted with this, said that Soldado João Vas had spoken of the premediated rebellion to the Deponent, but that the latter was not ready to believe this.[38]

Soldado Manoel de Aguiar

Relating to Soldado Manoel de Aguiar of the *Companhia de Freitas*, he stated that Cabo Ferrão had asked him to take an oath. He further said that the Cabo had told him that they would create six Legions and give posts of the Cabo to all. This was denied by Cabo Ferrão when questioned.[39]

Cabo Sebastião Dias

Cabo Sebastião Dias stated that Tenente Gonzaga had called him to tie a horse. He told him that they should gather all the Christian natives to kill the Portuguese. To this, Dias responded that their ancestors had not killed them, when they first came. The Tenente replied saying that the killing of the Portuguese was good, for then only the *Cabos das Esquadras* would become *Sargentos*, that *Sargentos* would become *Alferes* and from this to the level of *Tenentes*, *Capitaens* and *Coroneis*. Dias told him that whatever he said was not right and was not possible. As he had already tied the horse, the Tenente was moving out. At this stage, he asked Dias, whether he thought the issue he was referring to was a joke. The Cabo on reaching the *Quartel da Companhia* made a derogatory remark about Goan Brahmins. The Tenente did not take this lightly. He scolded the Cabo, to which Dias responded that he was referring to the other Brahmins and not to the Tenentes. Meanwhile Cabo Ferrão came towards the *Quartel* and Dias told him all that transpired between him and the Tenente. To which Cabo Ferrão replied that those were the mannerisms of the Brahmins.[40]

Soldado Xavier Dias

Soldado Xavier Dias of the *Companhia de Freitas* stated that he had no knowledge of the revolt.[41]

Soldado Fabião Alvares

On being questioned about his involvement in the conspiracy, Soldado Fabião Alvares categorically denied that he knew anything about the conspiracy. When confronted by Cabo Manoel Ferrão, who said that Tenente Gonzaga had told him that he had spoken to Alvares about the conspiracy, had invited him to join it and that he, Alvares had shown willingness to do so, Alvares totally denied this.[42]

Sargento Baltazar Caeiro

On being interrogated, Sargento Baltazar Caeiro on August 10, narrated what he knew about the conspiracy, fomented by Tenente Pedro Luis Gonzaga and Tenente Manoel Caetano Pinto. He replied that on August 5 (Sunday), the said Tenente Gonzaga, at the foot of the house of the *Brigadeiro* called out to him. Together they moved to Gonzaga's room. Tenente Manoel Caetano Pinto was present there. Both the Tenentes asked Caeiro if he could arrange 200 men in the village of Assolna. They said that in Assolna, the native place of Caeiro, there were men who were huge and were capable of dealing with the Portuguese. Would they be ready to rise against the Portuguese? Tenente Gonzaga further said that there would be six ships of an imperial nation, that they already had 200 Muslims on payment from outside the *Estado* and a lot of money. For all this, there was sanction from Rome. A native priest had come from Rome, stating that it was not a sin to stage the revolt. Tenente Gonzaga said further, that a native of Nagoa with the surname Noronha would come to Ponda with all the news which Caeiro did not know. Tenente Gonzaga stated that he wished to speak to Furriel Antonio Pedro, that he had won over the Cabo of his *Companhia*, Manoel Ferrão, Soldado Manoel de Aguiar and others, whose names he did not disclose. They were promised posts. In the presence of Caeiro, Tenente Gonzaga asked Cabo Manoel Ferrão if he was a *Portabandeira*. The latter confirmed this. When Sargento Caeiro expressed doubts relating to the uprising of the people, Tenente Gonzaga tried his best to allay his fears.[43]

Sargento Caeiro also declared that the *Ajudante de Cirurgia*, Francisco Pereira told him that the above said two Tenentes, had already spoken to him about the revolt. Both of them felt that this was nonsensical and that it was impossible to materalise. When faced with the deposition of Cabo Manoel Ferrão, who declared that Caeiro had told him that he had discussed the matter of the revolt with Furriel Antonio Pedro, the Sargento denied this. He declared further that Tenente Gonzaga explained to him, that the British Americans had revolted and established a Republic. They used signals for uniting the rebels. One night they took refuge in the churches so that parish priests could gather the people together and that unitedly they could throw off the British yoke and thus become free. Similarly, they had planned to send notices to all the parish priests, that they would ring the bells of the churches one night and when the people would gather, some letters would be read out, some particularly terrible ones, so as to convince the people, to unite to end the Portuguese rule.[44]

On August 11, 1787 Antonio de Asa Castello Branco reported to the authorities that he had taken steps to enquire into the denunciations made. He was of the opinion that almost all that Cabo Manoel Ferrão had deposed was without foundation. Cabo Ferrão had merely reported what Tenente Gonzaga had told him. He took great care to see that timely arrests were made and that no one had escaped. It was proven that Sargento Baltazar Caeiro, Cabo Manoel Ferrão, Cabo Antonio Fernandes and Soldado João Vas were involved in the said conspiracy. But this was not the case with Cirurgia mor David Francisco Viegas, as he was sick at home.[45]

Castello Branco also submitted to the authorities the denunciations of Fr. Francisco José de Jesus Maria, Cabo Manoel Ferrão and Cabo Antonio Fernandes, together with the counter-statements and cross-examination statements of those denonounced.[46]

On the Trail of The Fugitive

The authorities had succeeded in getting their hands on most of the rebels. But the chief organizer of the rebellion, Fr. José Antonio Gonsalves escaped their clutches. He very shrewdly staged his great escape. It seems that just as he had planned the revolt, he meticulously planned his escape. He knew that failure of any kind would amount to certain arrest and the harshest of punishments, as in the eyes of the Portuguese authorities, his activities amounted to sedition and high treason.

It would be relevant to trace the trail of the fugitive and the efforts of the Portuguese Government to capture him.

At Pilerne

On August 4, 1787 Fr. Gonsalves was at the house of Fr. Miguel Alvares, but after dinner he left, accompanied by the Italian, José Luis Guinete. Fr. Miguel had heard that he had spent that night at the home of a widow at Pilerne.[47] But according to the statement of Tomas Filipe Ribeiro, *Escrivão* of the *Senado de Bardez*, Fr. Gonsalves was a guest of Fr. José Manoel Ribeiro, at the house of his neighbour, in the beginning of August.[48]

On August 6, Fr. Gonsalves was invited for dinner at the house of Fr. Vicente Alvares. It was the occasion of the Feast of Harvest. There were others present for dinner—Geraldo Ferreira of Arpora, whose work was to arrange contractors for *communidade* fields, Fr. José Manoel Ribeiro and Fr. Rafael Marcos.[49] On the same day, a soldier from the Legion of Ponda, accompanied by a *cafre*, brought a letter for Fr. João Baptista Pinto. As he was not at home, the soldier moved to the house of Fr. Miguel Alvares. But Fr. Pinto was not there too. It was indeed a warning message for Fr. Gonsalves, as he had been denounced. Anticipating danger, he prepared to flee and left Pilerne that evening or in the early hours of August 7.[50]

Fr. Rafael Marcos, when questioned by the authorities stated that Fr. Gonsalves left the home of Fr. Vicente Alvares, saying that he was leaving for Piedade, which was indeed an enormous bluff.[51] But Micael Silvestre who had accompanied Fr. Gonsalves to Guirim stated that the latter left the house of Fr. Vicente Alvares to move to the house of his cousin who was the wife of Sargent-mor Miguel Alvares (?).[52]

According to Fr. Miguel Alvares, Vicar of the parish of Pilerne, on August 6, Fr. Gonsalves sent a message requesting him to meet him, which he obliged. Fr. Gonsalves told him that he was proceeding to Chorão and requested him to distribute amongst the poor, *contas* and *vernicas* (?) which he said had indulgences attached to them.[53]

On August 7, Major Henrique Claudio de Tonnelat arrived at the home of Fr. Vicente Alvares and enquired about the whereabouts of Fr. Gonsalves. To this, Fr. Alvares replied that

Fr. Gonsalves had been at his place for dinner the previous day, and that he left the same day.[54]

It appears from the trial records, that Fr. Gonsalves did not tell any of the other rebels, about the message of the premature disclosure of the proposed revolt and the denunciations made. He merely thought of saving his own skin. This is a classic case of the captain deserting his sinking ship. Otherwise, what explains the fact that other rebels were not able to escape arrests, specially those in Pilerne and neighbouring areas. Besides, he had spun tales to buy time to escape.

At Guirim

Fr. Gonsalves reached the Parochial House of the church of Guirim in the wee hours of August 7, accompanied by Micael Silvestre, a young boy from Pilerne. The latter claimed to be a relative of Fr. Miguel and Fr. Vicente Alvares.[55]

Fr. José Manoel Menezes, the Vicar of the church of Guirim was taken aback to see the said priest. He was dressed oddly, in white pants, slippers without socks, in a cloak and with his head covered with a handkerchief. He asked Fr. Gonsalves the reason for appearing in this strange manner. Fr. Gonsalves told him, that the *Vigario Geral* had issued orders for his arrest and he requested him to arrange a carriage.[56] To this, Fr. Menezes reacted saying that he could not permit him to stay in his house and that he should move to another place.

In all probability, Fr. Menezes made arrangements for Fr. Gonsalves to move to the home of Donato Antonio Vas. Around 11 o'clock in the morning, guided by a boy of the school of the church of Guirim, named Caetano de Souza, Fr. Gonsalves came to the house of Donato Antonio Vas. Fr. Menezes came later and behind him was a woman who brought food in a *cesto*. Fr. Menezes, Fr. Gonsalves, Donato Antonio Vas and another

Donato, who was a companion of the latter, had lunch together.[57] Fr. Menezes in his statement indicated that he had provided food to Fr. Gonsalves on humanitarian grounds.

Fr. Gonsalves kept saying several times that he had not committed any crime to make the Vicar General go against him. He wanted to go to Piedade to suspend the said order that was issued against him.

After lunch, Fr. Gonsalves and the boy Micael Silvestre, moved to the church and then waited outside for transportation. Only two *boias* turned up, which was not enough. Therefore they decided to undertake their journey on foot. Fr. Gonsalves however requested for a *cafre*.[58]

They reached the village of Sirula, where they met Vicente Lobo who took them to his house and offered them tea. Then the latter went to arrange an *almadia* (boat), in which Fr. Gonsalves in the evening of August 7, left for Chorão.[59]

On the next day quite early in the morning, the Capitão of the Legion, his officers and soldiers came in search of Fr. Gonsalves at Guirim. Fr. Menezes told them that Fr. Gonsalves had come to Guirim speaking of an order issued by *Vigario Geral*. He said further, that soon after lunch Fr. Gonsalves left, saying that he was proceeding to Chorão and from there to Piedade. The officials did not believe Fr. Menezes, and demanded that he should show them where he had taken refuge. Meanwhile another *Capitão* of the Legion arrived at the church of Guirim and began to question Fr. Menezes about Fr. Gonsalves. He once again explained, that the said priest told him that he would be proceeding to Sirula and from there to Chorão and Piedade. To this they replied, that he would not be able to move easily as the entire region was encircled by their *companhia* and because of the existence of a river. Moreover all the passages were blocked. There were orders from the Governor General to seize him. The house of Fr. Menezes was thoroughly searched and the officials thus ascertained that Fr. Gonsalves had gone away. They said that they would report everything to the *Coronel* of the Legion.[60]

At 5 o'clock in the evening, Fr. Menezes could write his report and it was taken by the *Capitão* who had been sent for the specific duty of capturing Fr. Gonsalves. On reaching Colvale, the officials reported the happenings, at Guirim, to the *Coronel* of the Legion of Bardez, as he was the competent authority as *Comandante de Province*.[61]

Fr. Menezes felt unhappy that he had not given a proper and accurate account of what happened. He felt that he should have done it on August 9. Instead he could do so only on August 10.[62] The *Capitão* was in Pilerne and he therefore delayed in his duty.

Fr. Menezes wrote to the *Ajudante Geral* on August 10, reporting all that had happened at Guirim with respect to Fr. Gonsalves. He further stated that he was totally ignorant of the arrests of others. He stated that if he had reported earlier, he would not be able to do it properly and diligently and if delayed further it would be a great crime because the matter was already denounced and proceedings were on relating to the guilty.[63]

On August 10, there arrived at the Parochial House at Guirim two soldiers of the *Tropa* in search of Fr. Gonsalves. Fr. Menezes told them that Fr. Gonsalves had come to Guirim, but had moved to Sirula.[64] He further told them, that Vicente Lobo of Sirula had provided an *almadia* for Fr. Gonsalves to move to Chorão. He told the Major that he was not aware of anything that had happened before the arrival of Fr. Gonsalves at Gurim.

On August 11, 1787 Fr. Menezes was once again questioned on the matter of Fr. Gonsalves. He repeated the same issues indicated above before *Sargento-mor Comandante de Campanhia de Cavalos* of the Province of Bardez. On August 23, 1787 Fr. Menezes was arrested.[65]

At Chorão

Fr. Gonsalves arrived at the house of Fr. Mathias Bernardo de Fonseca accompanied by Micael Silvestre and a *cafre*. Here too he was dressed oddly. Showing surprise, Fr. Fonseca enquired as to the reason for his appearance. To this Fr. Gonsalves replied that since it was raining, the weather demanded it. Fr. Fonseca invited him to stay for dinner. He told him categorically that he could not keep him at this house, as news was around that Fr. Gonsalves' brothers had been arrested. Fr. Gonsalves told Fr. Fonseca that there was a similar order for his arrest and that he wanted to occupy the vacant house of Roza Maria. He was told that the key to the said house was with Roza Maria's son Manoel.[66]

Fr. Fonseca, Fr. Gonsalves, Micael Silvestre, the *cafre* and Manoel moved towards the house of Roza Maria. On the way, Fr. Fonseca called out to Begarim Lourenço Fernandes and asked him to accompany them. On reaching the house of Roza Maria which was contiguous with that of Vicente de Abreu, a relative of Fr. Fonseca, Begarim Lourenço was sent to call Abreu. The latter met Fr. Gonsalves and they were in conversation for sometime.[67] As per the statement of Abreu to the authorities, Fr. Fonseca requested him to attend to the food arrangements of Fr. Gonsalves on grounds of friendship and humanitarianism.[68] But when cross examined Fr. Fonseca denied this.[69]

Fr. Fonseca then returned to his house, accompanied by Manoel, Micael Silvestre and Begarim Lourenço. The *cafre* remained with Fr. Gonsalves that night (August 7). In the subsequent days, Fr. Fonseca did not see Fr. Gonsalves as he was suffering from inflamation of the eyes.[70] Abreu provided food to Fr. Gonsalves for the next three days.[71]

Micael Silvestre, who had accompanied Fr. Gonsalves from Pilerne to Chorão in his statement said, that he found Fr. Gonsalves behaving in a strange way, like a fugitive and asked him why he was absconding. To this, Fr. Gonsalves responded that there was an order of the Archbishop to imprison him. While on the night of August 7, Fr. Gonsalves stayed in the vacant house, Silvestre took shelter in the house of Fr. Fonseca. The next morning Silvestre left for his coconut grove, which he possessed in the village of Chorão. On the next day he returned to the vacant house where the said priest Fr. Gonsalves was residing. After dinner, he returned back to his coconut grove where he spent some days and then returned to Pilerne.[72] He later came to know about the conspiracy and the arrests of several priests and persons.

Vicente de Abreu in his deposition indicated that Fr. Fonseca sent a message to him through Begarim Lourenço to get rid off Fr. Gonsalves at the earliest, that any delay would be prejudicial to them. This was perhaps because of the arrests of the priests implicated in the aborted revolt or because he could not manage the expenses.[73] This was totally denied by Fr. Fonseca when questioned.[74]

According to Joana, commonly known as Fillu, one night Fr. Mathias and Begarim Lourenço went to the house of Vicente de Abreu and made her take an oath not to disclose that the said priest and the said Begarim had ever come to the house of Vicente de Abreu.[75]

There were three *begarins*, namely Vicente Gomes, Vitorino Vas and Filipe Fernandes who were employed to take Fr. Gonsalves out of the *Estado* and guide him to Azarem in the land of the Marathas. This arrangement was made by Vicente de Abreu. For this work they were promised 15 *xerafins* each and that the payment would be made on reaching Azarem. Vitorino Vas stated to the authorities when questioned that he received only one *rupia*.[76] Filipe Fernandes said he did not receive anything.[77] Vicente de Abreu totally denied his involvement. Instead he said that Fr. Gonsalves had taken with him 75 *xerafins* of which six *rupias* he gave to Begarim Filipe.[78] The trial records also reveal that Fr. Menezes had given 25 *rupias* to Fr. Gonsalves for some theological work.[79]

At the time when Fr. Gonsalves was at Chorão, José Caetano Gomes of Piedade was called to Chorão. A message was sent through a woman called Maria de Sequeira.[80] According to Abreu he was called for the purpose of handling the purchase of a coconut grove.[81]

Fr. Gonsalves, José Caetano Gomes and Vicente de Abreu had dinner together. A discussion took place about the arrests. Fr. Gonsalves stated that his brother Manoel Francisco was arrested for having gone beyond *do citado a algum serviço* and his other brother Fr. Luis Antonio, for some debts. When he was told that perhaps there were orders for his arrest, he said he suspected this, and wanted to speak to the Governor General. This episode was reported by José Caetano Gomes in his statement during the trial.

Gomes said further, that during the entire duration of the *cea* (supper), he saw three *begarins* outside the house consuming wine.[82] That same night Fr. Gonsalves left (August 11, 1787) and before leaving he took out some *calões* from a wardrobe. According to Gomes while doing so, some *rupias* and *pardaus* fell to the ground and he (Gomes) picked them up and handed them to Fr. Gonsalves. But some people felt, that Gomes had given some money to Fr. Gonsalves which was sent by his sister-in-law, wife of Manoel Francisco.[83]

Both José Caetano Gomes and Vicente de Abreu accompanied Fr. Gonsalves to the patio of the house. A ship was ordered to stand by. The priest embarked saying that he was on his way to meet His Excellency, the Governor General. Gomes observed that it was very late and therefore returned to the house of Vicente de Abreu and left the following morning.[84]

Fr. Gonsalves had remained in hiding for about four days at the vacant house of Rosa Maria. He found sanctuary in the desolate village of Chorão and the authorities were totally ignorant of this. He had the gall to hoodwink them. He not only remained in hiding in Chorão, but also moved to Azarem. He successfully crossed the borders of the *Estado da India* and reached Maratha territory. He kept his movements secret and concocted clever cover stories.

According to Fr. Fonseca, he did know about the arrests of the brothers of Fr. Gonsalves, but did not know the reasons for the same. He learnt about them on August 9, 1787. It was Fr. Joaquim Bernardo Albuquerque, who told him that the said brothers were arrested, because together with other natives they planned to stage a revolt against the Portuguese and that Fr. Gonsalves was a fugitive for this reason. Fr. Fonseca stated that he was able to confirm this only on August 14.[85]

But Fr. Albuquerque in his testimony said that Fr. Fonseca came to him on August 7 at the church of Nossa Senhora da Graça saying that the brothers of Fr. Gonsalves of Piedade had been arrested and no one seemed to know the reason why this happened. He further told Fr. Albuquerque that they might have been arrested because with others they had planned a revolt against the *Estado*.[86]

Fr. Fonseca further said that on August 9, Xavier Mendonça Corte Real, a resident of Chorão, was assigned the duty of searching for Fr. Gonsalves. Corte Real did not meet Fr. Fonseca and therefore the latter did not consider it his obligation to disclose the whereabouts of Fr. Gonsalves, that he was in hiding in the house of Roza Maria.[87]

Vicente de Abreu was aware of the arrests of the brothers of Fr. Gonsalves and other priests, at the time when the latter was at his home. But Fr. Gonsalves told him that this was because of the orders of the *Arcebispo Primaz* because it was felt in Portugal that Fr. Gonsalves wanted to be the Archbishop of Goa. Abreu further questioned Fr. Gonsalves about it, who told him, that when he was in Portugal, a request of *Camara de Bardez* had reached the Queen that Fr. Gonsalves be considered for the post of Archbishop of Goa. The priests were therefore arrested on the instructions that came from Portugal.[88]

Micael Silvestre, the boy from Pilerne, who had accompanied Fr. Gonsalves right upto Chorão, later came to know about the conspiracy and the arrests of several secular and religious persons for sedition, and that for this reason Fr. Gonsalves was on the run. He learnt that the officials were on the search for the said priest. He therefore went to make a denunciation before Major Henrique Claudio de Tonnelat. He stated that he had no knowledge of the conspiracy and declared all that happened since he met Fr. Gonsalves. When at the house of Vicente Lobo, Fr. Gonsalves spoke loudly and publicly and never in a suspicious manner, but at the house of Fr. Mathias, he spoke in a secretive manner.[89]

Begarim Lourenço Fernandes stated that during the entire period when Fr. Gonsalves was on the island of Chorão, he had learnt of the arrests of some priests, but did not know the reason for the same. He was told by the authorities to speak the truth as Fr. Gonsalves was in the house of Rosa Maria for 3 to 4 days and the arrests had taken place 4 to 5 days before. To this Lourenço replied that he was an ordinary man, a rustic, and did not know anything at that point of time.[90]

Begarim Filipe Fernandes stated that only when he took Fr. Gonsalves outside the *Estado*, that he had heard of the arrests of some priests, but he had not heard of the severity of their crimes nor that Fr. Gonsalves was involved in it. The said priest told him that he was going for missionary work to the Maratha territories.[91]

The *begarins* – Vicente Gomes, Vitorino Vas and Filipe Fernandes had guided Fr. Gonsalves along interior and remote roads. They moved hidingly and had not met anyone, right upto the lands outside the *Estado da India*. All of them categorically told the authorities when questioned, that they became aware of the arrests of the natives of Goa because of an attempted revolt, only when they were outside the *Estado* or when they returned back to Chorão. [92]

When Fr. Gonsalves learnt that the revolt had been leaked and denounced, he fled. Inspite of all the efforts of the Governor General, the wily priest escaped arrest.

The Governor General issued orders, that the people of Goa were forbidden from rendering any help to the said priest, on pain of penalty of imprisonment. He announced, by the *Bando* of August 21, 1787 an amount of 5000 *xerafins* for anyone who would capture and hand over the fugitive to the Government.[93] These efforts proved futile. The fugitive was never captured.

Sipais were sent by the Portuguese Government to bring back the rebel. The soldiers entered into negotiations with the Maratha Sarkar who was filled with ambition. The soldiers too had their eyes on the 5000 *xerafins* promised by the Government. They succeeded in arresting Fr. Gonsalves. But while returning through Azarem, Fr. Gonsalves shouted for help. The Christians there, came to his assistance.

It appeared that a Brahmin, named Babu Rao governed the said village of Azarem. [94] Desperate to negotiate the release of Fr. Gonsalves, the Portuguese Government sent a *Tenente Cabo de Sipaes*, with a *cedula* in which it was promised that 5000 *xerafins* would be given in the name of His Majesty, the King of Portugal to Babu Rao for the rebel. It was a way of placing a bait before him, whether he was interested in the prize money and wished to be free of negotiation with Pune. [95]

Another *Cabo*, Hindu by origin, was sent to see if he could succeed with the said Brahmin. But the authorities would not release Fr. Gonsalves without orders from Pune.[96]

An emissary was sent to Pune to plead the release of Fr. Gonsalves who was a criminal of the Portuguese Government. He reminded them of a similar situation that took place and what was practiced in the case of the handing over of Tulagi Ponvar in 1780. Accordingly, orders were issued by Vencat Rau Naraina, of the Pune Government, to the Governor of the jurisdiction, directing him to release Fr. Gonsalves and to hand him over to the Portuguese.[97]

The Portuguese authorities sent an official with *sipaes* to Azarem to show the orders and to arrest Fr. Gonsalves. But they were informed that Fr. Gonsalves was not at Azarem and that he had moved on to Ixalcargi. Accordingly, the official was called back. The Portuguese Government looked upon this, as a breach of trust on the part of the *Potencias Asiaticas*.

It was discovered that a few days before the handing over, the Government of the said jurisdiction, allowed Fr. Gonsalves to proceed to Ixalcargi.[98] The Brahmin of Azarem was given two days by the Portuguese official to resolve the issue, to write to the Governor of the jurisdiction of Ixalcargi. Despite all this, they did not hand over, the said Fr. José Antonio Gonsalves.

With this news, the Goa Government ordered its emissary in Pune to follow up the matter and to see to the effective handing over of the said rebel. He was told that the outcome of all this was being awaited.[99]

But the truth is that despite attempts and efforts made from August 8, 1787 to January 1788, Fr. José Antonio Gonsalves, the chief ringleader of the aborted revolt of 1787 by some strange fate, succeeded in escaping from the clutches of the Portuguese Government, was temporarily offered asylum in Maratha territory and perhaps never ever returned back to Goa.[100] He displayed an uncanny knack for surviving the most devastating setbacks. Fr. Gonsalves had the nerve to undertake his escape so calculatingly, leave aside succeed at it. He was able to pull off an extraordinary feat and cheat death at the gallows. For this too he should be remembered.

REFERENCES

1. AHU : *MI* Maço 155(153), Letter of Sebastião José Ferreira Barroco to Martinho Melo e Castro and Francisco da Cunha Menezes, doc. dtd. 9 Aug. 1787.
2. AHU : *MI* Maço 155(153). Letter of Francisco da Cunha Menezes, doc. dtd. 9 Aug. 1787.
3. AHU : *MI* Maço 155(153), doc. dtd. Oct. 1787
4. HAG : *MR* 170, fls. 23v-24.
5. HAG : *MR* 169A, fl. 205
6. AHU : *MI* Maço 155(153), doc. dtd. 15 Dec. 1787
7. AHU : *MI* Maço 155(153), doc. dtd. 9 Aug. 1787
8. AHU : *MI* Maço 155(153), doc. dtd. 17 Jan. 1788.
9. AHU : *MI* Maço 155(153), Letter of Sebastião José Ferreira Barroco, doc. dtd. 9 Aug. 1787; Letter of Francisco da Cunha Menezes, doc. dtd. 9 Aug. 1787.
10. AHU : *MI* Maço 155(153), doc. dtd. 11 Aug. 1787.
11. AHU : *MI* Maço 155(153), doc. dtd. 11 Aug. 1787.
12. AHU : *MI* Maço 155(153), doc. dtd. 11 Aug. 1787.
13. AHU : *MI* Maço 155(153), Devassa, Auto No. 44, Statement of Caetano da Costa.
14. AHU : *MI* Maço 155(153), Devassa, Testemunha Referida, Statement of José.
15. AHU : *MI* Maço 155(153), Letter of José Antonio Pinto to Fr. João Baptista Pinto, doc. dtd. 15 March, 1787.
16. AHU : *MI* Maço 155(153), Letters of Eloy José Correia Peixoto to Fr. José Antonio Gonsalves, docs. dtd. 15 Sept. 1786; 20 March 1787; Letter of Joaquim Antonio Vicente to Fr. José Antonio Gonslaves, doc. dtd. 20 Sept. 1786.
17. AHU : *MI* Maço 155(153), docs. dtd. 15 Sept. 1786; 20 March 1787.
18. AHU : *MI* Maço 155(153), doc. dtd 15 March, 1787.
19. AHU : *MI* Maço 155(153), doc. dtd 15 March, 1787.
20. AHU : *MI* Maço 155(153), doc. dtd. 20 Sept. 1786.
21. AHU : *MI* Maço 155(153), doc. dtd. 20 Sept. 1786.
22. AHU : *MI* Maço 155(153), doc. dtd. 20 Sept. 1786; Denunciation of Fr. José de Jesus Maria, doc. dtd. 8 Aug. 1787.
23. AHU : *MI* Maço 155(153), Statement of Francisco Pereira, doc. dtd. 8 Aug.
24. AHU : *MI* Maço 155(153), Denunciation of Antonio Fernandes, doc. dtd. 9 Aug. 1787.

25. AHU : *MI* Maço 155(153), Deposition of Cabo Manoel Ferrão doc. dtd. 11 Aug. 1787.
26. AHU : *MI* Maço 155(153), Deposition of Antonio Pereira
27. AHU : *MI* Maço 155(153), Deposition of Simões.
28. AHU : *MI* Maço 155(153), Deposition of Joaquim Barreto.
29. AHU : *MI* Maço 155(153), Deposition of Miguel Gaunço
30. AHU : *MI* Maço 155(153), Deposition of José Gracias
31. AHU : *MI* Maço 155(153), Deposition of Pedro da Roza
32. AHU : *MI* Maço 155(153), Deposition of Vitorino Simões.
33. AHU : *MI* Maço 155(153), Deposition of Avelino Antonio Soares.
34. AHU : *MI* Maço 155(153), Deposition of Manoel Pereira
35. AHU : *MI* Maço 155(153), Deposition of Pascoal Antonio
36. AHU : *MI* Maço 155(153), Deposition of José Vas
37. AHU : *MI* Maço 155(153), Deposition of João Vas
38. AHU : *MI* Maço 155(153), Deposition of Antonio Rodrigues
39. AHU : *MI* Maço 155(153), Deposition of Manoel de Aguiar
40. AHU : *MI* Maço 155(153), Deposition of Sebastião Dias
41. AHU : *MI* Maço 155(153), Deposition of Xavier Dias
42. AHU : *MI* Maço 155(153), Deposition of Fabião Alvares
43. AHU : *MI* Maço 155(153), Deposition of Baltazar Caeiro, doc. dtd. 10 Aug. 1787.
44. AHU : *MI* Maço 155(153), Deposition of Baltazar Caeiro, doc. dtd. 10 Aug. 1787.
45. AHU : *MI* Maço 155(153), doc. dtd. 11 Aug. 1787.
46. AHU : *MI* Maço 155(153), doc. dtd. 11 Aug. 1787.
47. AHU : *MI* Maço 155(153), Devassa, Auto No. 8, Statement of Fr. Miguel Alvares.
48. AHU : *MI* Maço 155(153), Devassa, Witness No. 14, Statement of Tomas Filipe Ribeiro.
49. AHU : *MI* Maço 155(153), Devassa, Auto No. 14, Statement of Fr. Vicente Alvares.
50. AHU : *MI* Maço 155(153), Devassa Witness No. 32, Statement of Micael Silvestre.
51. AHU : *MI* Maço 155(153), Devassa, Witness No. 33, Statement of Fr. Rafael Marcos.
52. AHU : *MI* Maço 155(153), Devassa, Witness No. 32. Statement of Micael Silvestre.
53. AHU : *MI* Maço 155(153), Devassa, Auto No. 9, Statement of Fr. Miguel Alvares.
54. AHU : *MI* Maço 155(153), Devassa, Auto No. 14, Statement of Fr. Vicente Alvares.
55. AHU : *MI* Maço 155(153), Devassa, Witness No. 32, Statement of Micael Silvestre.
56. AHU : *MI* Maço 155(153), Devassa, No. Auto 19, Statement of Fr. José Manoel de Menezes doc. dtd. 19 Nov. 1787.
57. AHU : *MI* Maço 155(153), Devassa, Witness No. 29, Statement of Antonio José Paes; Witness No. 31, Statement of Antonio Vas; Testemunha Referida, Statement of Rosa; Witness No. 31, Statement of Antonio Vas; Testemunha Referida, Statement Caetano de Souza; Witness No. 32, Statement of Micael Silvestre.
58. AHU : *MI* Maço 155(153), Statement of Fr. José Manoel Menezes, doc. dtd. 19 Nov. 1787.
59. AHU : *MI* Maço 155(153), Witness No. 32, Statement of Micael Silvestre.

60. AHU : *MI* Maço 155(153), Statement of Fr. José Manoel Menezes, doc. dtd. 19 Nov. 1787.
61. AHU : *MI* Maço 155(153), Statement of Fr. José Manoel Menezes, doc. dtd. 19 Nov. 1787.
62. AHU : *MI* Maço 155(153), Statement of Fr. José Manoel Menezes, doc. dtd. 19 Nov. 1787.
63. AHU : *MI* Maço 155(153), Statement of Fr. José Manoel de Menezes, doc dtd. 19 Nov. 1787.
64. AHU : *MI* Maço 155(153), Devassa, Auto No. 19, Statement of Fr. José Manoel de Menezes; doc. dtd. 19 Nov. 1787.
65. AHU : *MI* Maço 155(153), Statement of Fr. José Manoel de Menezes, doc. dtd. 19 Nov. 1787; Auto No. 19, Statement of Fr. José Manoel de Menezes.
66. AHU : *MI* Maço 155(153), Devassa, Auto No.12, Statement of Fr. Mathias Bernardo da Fonseca.
67. AHU : *MI* Maço 155(153), Devassa, Auto No.12, Statement of Fr. Mathias Bernardo da Fonseca.
68. AHU : *MI* Maço 155(153), Devassa, Auto No.1, Statement of Vicente de Abreu.
69. AHU : *MI* Maço 155(153), Devassa, Auto No.12, Statement of Fr. Mathias Bernardo da Fonseca.
70. AHU : *MI* Maço 155(153), Devassa, Auto No.12, Statement of Fr. Mathias Bernardo da Fonseca.
71. AHU : *MI* Maço 155(153), Devassa, Auto No.12, Statement of Fr. Mathias Bernardo da Fonseca.
72. AHU : *MI* Maço 155(153), Devassa, Witness No. 32, Statement of Micael Silvestre.
73. AHU : *MI* Maço 155(153), Devassa, Auto No.1, Statement of Vicente de Abreu.
74. AHU : *MI* Maço 155(153), Devassa, Auto No.12, Statement of Fr. Mathias Bernardo da Fonseca.
75. AHU : *MI* Maço 155(153), Devassa, Testemunha Referida, Statement of Joana (Fillu) de Souza.
76. AHU : *MI* Maço 155(153), Devassa, Auto No.38, Statement of Vitorino Vas.
77. AHU : *MI* Maço 155(153), Devassa, Auto No. 39, Statement of Filipe Fernandes
78. AHU : *MI* Maço 155(153), Devassa, Auto No.1, Statement of Vicente de Abreu.
79. AHU : *MI* Maço 155(153), Devassa, Auto No.12, Statement of Fr. Mathias Bernardo da Fonseca
80. AHU : *MI* Maço 155(153), Devassa, Testemunha Referida, Statement of Maria de Siqueira
81. AHU : *MI* Maço 155(153), Devassa, Auto No.1, Statement of Vicente de Abreu.
82. AHU : *MI* Maço 155(153), Devassa, Witness 28, Statement of José Caetano Gomes; HAG: *MR* 169A, fls. 207v-208v.
83. AHU : *MI* Maço 155(153), Devassa, Witness 28, Statement of José Caetano Gomes; HAG: *MR* 169A, fls. 207v-208v.
84. AHU : *MI* Maço 155(153), Devassa, Witness 28, Statement of José Caetano Gomes.
85. AHU : *MI* Maço 155(153), Devassa, Auto No.12, Statement of Fr. Mathias Bernardo da Fonseca.

86. AHU : *MI* Maço 155(153), Devassa, Testemunha Referida, Statement of Fr. Joaquim Bernardo de Albuquerque.
87. AHU : *MI* Maço 155(153), Devassa, Auto No.12, Statement of Fr. Mathias Bernardo da Fonseca.
88. AHU : MI Maço 155(153), Devassa, Auto No.1, Statement of Vicente de Abreu.
89. AHU : *MI* Maço 155(153), Devassa, Witness No.32, Statement of Micael Silvestre
90. AHU : *MI* Maço 155(153), Devassa, Auto No. 40, Statement of Lourenço Fernandes.
91. AHU : *MI* Maço 155(153), Devassa, Auto No. 39, Statement of Filipe Fernandes
92. AHU : *MI* Maço 155(153), Devassa, Auto No. 37, Statement of Vicente Gomes; Auto No. 38, Statement of Vitorino Vas; Auto No. 39, Filipe Fernandes; Auto No. 40, Lourenço Fernandes.
93. HAG: *MR* 169A, fl. 207.
94. HAG: *MR* 169A, fl. 207v.
95. HAG: *MR* 169A, fls. 207v-208v.
96. HAG: *MR* 169A, fl. 208.
97. HAG: *MR* 169A, fl. 208v.
98. HAG: *MR* 169A, fls. 208v-209.
99. HAG: *MR* 169A, fl. 209; AHU: *MI* Maço 155(153), doc. dtd. 17 Jan.1788.
100. Charles Borges, ed. *Goa and the Revolt of 1787*, p.68.

10

OFFICIAL REACTION AND RESPONSE: TRIAL AND SENTENCE

The attempt of the natives of Goa to end the Portuguese rule in 1787, and to establish a government of their choice, was indeed viewed seriously by the Portuguese authorities. It was not just a breach of law but a "*crime de Leza Majestade de Primeira Cabeça*". Steps were therefore taken to proceed with a thorough investigation into what what was termed as a criminal act of the highest order. By the *Carta* dated August 9,1787 José Joaquim de Sequeira Magalhaens e Lançöes, *Dezembargader do Paço and Chancelor do Estado*, was appointed the judicial authority to conduct the trial proceedings. Sebastião José Ferreira Barroco, Dezembargador of the *Relação de Goa* had to serve as *Escrivão*.[1] He had to *autasse* the said *Carta*, the denunciations made, a list of the accused (*reos*), a *summario* of witnesses prepared by *Vigario Geral* of the *Arcebispado* and other papers handed over, as per the Order received, to form the "*corpo de delicto*".[2] The interrogation of the accused and the witnesses was to be in keeping with the following *interrogatorios* issued on August 12, 1787.[3]

Article 1

Whether he knew that various natives of the land intended to stage a revolt to throw out of the *Estado* all the Portuguese generally called whites; who were the leaders and the members or accomplices of said revolt; and if in it, was any help of any *potencia.*

Article 2

Whether he knew Fr. José Antonio Gonsalves, also known by another name, José Filipe Gonsalves, resident of Piedade, Fr Caetano da Silva, Vicar of S. Lourenço de Linhares, Fr. José Vas, resident of Anjuna, Fr. Caetano Francisco de Couto.

Article 3

Whether at anytime he had spoken to the said persons and if he had heard them protest that they were oppressed by the Portuguese, if they had advanced any propositions that signified a desire to stage a revolt to became rulers and lords of the entire land.

Article 4

Whether he had seen the said priests holding meetings (*assembleas*) repeatedly in the Parochial House of the parish of Pilerne or at any other place and who were the members (*socios*) who joined them in the said meetings.

Article 5

Whether he knew the period taken by the said conspirators to plot the revolt.

Article 6

Whether he knew the means and methods that were adopted by the said conspirators.

Article 7

Whether he knew an Italian who was in the house of the Vicar of Pilerne, what was his nature and worth, how long was he in the land, why was he brought and did he join the said meetings.

Article 8

Whether he knew which conspirators had wealth and from where it came and if it was promised to anyone in order to enter the conspiracy.

Article 9

Whether he knew if the conspirators had with them men with hidden arms within the *Estado* with the intention of using them for a revolution that they had been hatching.

Article 10

Whether he know that the conspirators had robbed from some firms of the Governor General of the *Estado*.

Article 11

Whether he know that the conspirators had bribed the bakers to poison the bread and to prepare some drink to intoxicate the troops or part of them.

Article 12

Whether he knew that some officials of the two legions of Ponda and Bardez had been members and were party to the conspiracy; whether they had communicated with the natives in military forces.

The Jury began its sessions of examining witnesses on August 13, 1787. It examined and cross-examined 41 witnesses as per the *interrogatorios* stated above.[4] Witnesses No.1 was none other than the informer, Antonio Eugenio Toscano, brother of Tenente Inacio Toscano. Some of the other witnesses were :-

1) David Francisco Viegas, Cirurgião mor of the Legion of Ponda.
2) Henrique Claudio Tonnelat, Sargento Mor da Cavalaria
3) Sebastião de Noronha, Cabo da prayas of the province of Bardez
4) Fr. Daniel de Albuquerque, Curate of the church of Penha de França
5) Sebastião de Souza
6) Fr. Pedro Caetano José Lobo, Vicar of the church of Tivim
7) Fr. Baltazar Rodrigues of the church of Tivim
8) Fr. Vicente Filipe Coutinho of Aldona
9) Fr. Inacio Xavier Monis of Aldona
10) Caetano Correa, Sacristan of the church of Pilerne
11) José Caetano, Mestre of the church of Pomburpa
12) Andre Borges, Sacristan of the church of Pomburpa
13) Tomas Filipe Rodrigues, Escrivão of the Senado de Bardez
14) Miguel Francisco Xavier de Souza, Mestre of the church of Pilerne
15) José Caetano Gomes
16) Antonio José Paes, Sacristan of the church of Guirim
17) Xavier de Mendonça Corte Real, Fidalgo da Caza de Sua Magestade Capitão de Mar e Guerra.
18) Antonio Vas, Donato de S. Francisco of Guirim.
19) Micael Silvestre, of Chorão, resident of Pilerne.
20) Fr. Rafael Marcos, native of Chorão, resident of Pilerne
21) Antonio Filisberte da Silva of the church of Moira
22) Francisco Pereira, Sacristan of the church of Moira
23) José Soares of the church of Moira
24) Pedro Feraz (?), Cook of the Vicar of Moira
25) Fr. Francisco José de Souza, Presbitero, native of Moira.
26) Fr. Pedro de Souza, Presbitero do Habito de São Pedro, of Moira
27) Caetano de Couto of Panjim, relative of Fr. Couto
28) José Antonio de Lima, Alferes of the Legion of Ponda

In addition to the forty-one witnesses, there were other witnesses cross-examined, based on *referimentos*. The following is a list of *testmunhas referidas* (Table 10.1)

Table 10.1

LIST OF *TESTEMUNHAS REFERIDAS*

Sr.No.	Name	Remarks
1.	Rosa	Slave of Josepha Maria Gonsalves, sister-in-law of the Vicar of Guirim
2.	Rosa de Souza	Widow of Vicente Madeira of Chorão
3.	Caetano de Souza	13 years of age, from Guirim
4.	Fr. Mestre Filipe de Melo	*Clero Regular* of the *Congregação de Oratorio*, native of Santa Anna
5.	Maria de Sequeira	Widow of Thome Fernandes of Chorão
6.	Tomas Antonio Pereira	*Escrivão* of the village of Tivim
7.	Avelino Lourenço Lobo	Native of Sirula, resident of the City of Goa
8.	Fr. Caetano Antonio Lobo	Vicar of Reys Magos
9.	José Caetano Lobo	Resident of Serula, Bairro Velotim
10.	Geraldo Ferreira	Resident of Arpora
11.	Marcelino de Noronha	*Ajudante de Cirurgia*, Legion of Ponda
12.	Fr. Joaquim Bernardo de Albuquerque	Of Chorão; belonging to *Habito São Pedro*
13.	Matheus Mendes	Cabo da Esquadra, Legion of Pond
14.	Inacio Dias	*Soldado*, Legion of Ponda
15.	Joanna (Fillu)	Widow of João de Souza of Chorão
16.	Joaquim José	Of Santa Anna; *vargeiro*
17.	Rama Sinay	Businessman of Panjim
18.	Manoel Antonio de Oliveira Pontes	Capitão of the *Legião dos Voluntarios Reaes de Ponda*
19.	Filipe José Telles	*Sargento* of Legion of Ponda
20.	José Preto	Cook of Nagoa, Verna

Source : AHU: *MI* Maço 155(153), Devassa: *passim*.

It was certified that efforts were made to search for Manoel de Aguiar, Soldado, Legion of Ponda, *testemunha referida* by Baltazar Caeiro. Brigadeiro Antonio de Assa Castel Branco, Comandante of the said Legion was informed that the Soldado had fled from Panjim, and could not be traced.[5]

From the above it is clear that amongst the witnesses interrogated, a large number of them belonged to the staff attached to churches, like cooks, helpers, sacristans, curates etc. This helped to establish whether the rebels held meetings at the Parochial Houses, who were present there, what was discussed, particularly the role of Fr. Gonsalves, Fr. Couto, Fr. Pinto, the Vicars and the Tenentes of Bardez and Ponda. A picture of the manner in which Fr. Gonsalves escaped particularly his presence in Pilerne, Guirim and Chorão from August 6 till the day he fled to Maratha territory, could be also painted.

A large number of persons were questioned from in and around Panjim, specially neighbours, relatives and friends for details of the meetings held at the residence of Fr. Couto specially the meetings with Sebastião de Noronha. Likewise a lot of witnesses were cross-examined relating to the role of the Legion of Ponda particularly that of Tenente Gonzaga and Tenente Manoel Caetano Pinto.

The trial of the forty-six arrested and accused persons began on August 10, 1787. It began with Vicente de Abreu and ended with Narba Naique on December 5, 1787. Table 10.2 indicates the list of the said 46 accused persons and the dates of their respective jury sessions.

Table 10.2

CHARGED PERSONS / ACCUSED

Sr. No.	Charged Person	Date of Jury Session
1.	Vicente de Abreu	10 Aug. 1787
2.	Jose Luis (Italian)	5 Sept. 1787
3.	Fr. Caetano da Silva	6 Sept. 1787
4.	Fr. Manoel da Expectação	7 Sept. 1787
5.	Fr. João Alvares de Souza	11 (?) Sept. 1787
6.	Inacio Caetano Toscano	10 Sept. 1787
7.	Fr. Antonio Filipe Vas	13 (?) Sept. 1787
8.	Fr. Miguel Alvares	18 Sept. 1787
9.	Francisco Pereira	17 Oct. (?) 1787
10.	Nicolao Luis da Costa	19 Sept. 1787
11.	Fr. Caetano Francisco de Couto	26 Sept. 1787
12.	Fr. Mathias Bernardo da Fonseca	27 Sept. 1787
13.	Fr. Luis Antonio Gonsalves	1 Oct. 1787
14.	Fr. Vicente Alvares	3 Oct. 1787
15.	Baltazar Caeiro	3 Oct. 1787
16.	Antonio Fernandes	4 Oct. 1787
17.	Manoel Ferrão	4 Oct. 1787
18.	Luis Caetano de Souza	5 & 16 Oct. 1787
19.	Fr. José Manoel de Menezes	8 Oct. 1787
20.	Fr. José Antonio Vas	9 Oct. 1787
21.	Salvador Alvares da Costa	13 Oct. 1787
22.	Fr. João Baptista Pinto	15 Oct. 1787
23.	João Vas	17 Oct. 1787
24.	Pedro Luis Gongaga	?
25.	Manoel Luis	21 Oct. 1787
26.	Manoel Caetano Pinto	22 Oct. 1787

27.	David Francisco Viegas	24 Oct. 1787
28.	João de Souza Onorcar	5 Nov. 1787
29.	Sebastião de Noronha	20 & 22 Nov. 1787
30.	Fr. Sebastião Baptista	20 (?) Nov. 1787
31.	Manoel Pinto	20 Nov. 1787
32.	José Monteiro	21 Nov. 1787
33.	Bernardo de Misquita	21 Nov. 1787
34.	Pascoal Lazaro	22 Nov.1787
35.	Inacio Caetano Lopes	21 & 26 Nov. 1787
36.	Fr. Diogo Benedito Lobo	22 Nov. 1787
37.	Vicente Gomes	23 Nov. 1787
38.	Vitorino Vas	23 Nov. 1787
39.	Lourenço Fernandes	23 Nov. 1787
40.	Fr. Pedro Dalgado	23 Nov. 1787
41.	Filipe Fernandes	23 Nov, 1787
42.	Tomas Antonio Dias	26 Nov. 1787
43.	Fr. Jorge Dias	26 Nov. 1787
44.	Caetano Xavier da Costa	27 (?) Nov. 1787
45.	Miguel Antonio da Costa	27 Nov. 1787
46.	Narba Naique	5 Dec 1787

Source : AHU: *MI* Maço 155(153), Devassa: *passim*.

The Devassa records indicate that the examination of witnesses ended on December 10, 1787 and that of the charged persons/accused on December 5, 1787. It is thus evident that the examination of witnesses was conducted simultaneously with that of the accused. It is however strange that the judicial inquiry on Vicente de Abreu began on August 10, 1787 unless the document is wrongly dated.

Trial Proceedings

Those who categorically denied knowledge of the proposed revolt were :-[6]

1. Vicente de Abreu
2. José Luis Guinete, the Italian
3. Fr. Caetano da Silva
4. Fr. Manoel da Expectação
5. Fr. João Alvares de Souza
6. Fr. Antonio Filipe Vas
7. Fr. Miguel Alvares
8. Fr. Mathais Bernardo da Fonseca
9. Fr. Luis Antonio Gonsalves
10. Fr. Vicente Alvares
11. Fr. José Manoel de Menezes
12. Fr. João Baptista Pinto
13. Tenente Pedro Luis Gonzaga
14. Manoel Luis
15. Tenente Manoel Caetano Pinto
16. João de Souza Onorcar
17. Fr. Sebastião Baptista
18. Manoel Pinto
19. José Monteiro
20. Bernardo de Misquita
21. Pascoal Lazaro
22. Inacio Caetano Lopes, Capitão
23. Vicente Gomes
24. Vitorino Vas
25. Lourenço Fernandes
26. Fr. Pedro Dalgado
27. Filipe Fernandes
28. Tomas Antonio Dias
29. Miguel Antonio da Costa
30. Narba Naique
31. Fr. Jorge Dias

Those who admited knowledge of the proposed revolt were:-[7]

1. Fr. Diego Benedicto Lobo
2. Tenente Inacio Caetano Toscano
3. Francisco Pereira, Ajudante de Cirurgia
4. Tenente Nicolao Luis da Costa
5. Fr. Caetano Francisco de Couto
6. Sargento Baltazar Caeiro
7. Cabo Antonio Fernandes
8. Cabo Manoel Ferrão
9. Fr. Luis Caetano de Souza
10. Fr. José Antonio Vas
11. Salvador Alvares da Costa
12. João Vas, Soldado
13. David Francisco Viegas
14. Sebastião de Noronha
15. Caetano Xavier da Costa

Why Denunciations were made

From the trial proceedings and records, some reasons are obvious to us as to why denunciations were made. The main reason was the distrust that existed amongst the rebels whether clergy or military. There was the fear that others would denounce first and thereby implicate and incriminate them. Each of them desired to save his own skin. This is evident from the testimony of Tenente Inacio Caetano Toscano.[8]

Another significant reason was grudge and enemity. From Toscano's statement to the authorities, we gather that there was some kind of grudge between Fr. José Vas and Toscano's brother.

Fr. Manoel da Expectação had bad blood with Capitão Bernardo José Freitas who had challenged him on one occasion. For this, the priest had reprimanded him. He told him that he could be excommunicated and prohibited from entering the church. Fr. Expectação also declared that Fr. Arcanjo, Chaplain of the said

Legion was his enemy. [9] In all probality this enemity was behind the denunciations against Fr.Expectação.

Why Denunciations were not made

Several individuals were questioned by the authorities that though they were not party to the plot to overthrow the Portuguese regime in the *Estado da India* , yet when they had knowledge of it, why they did not denounce the same. Some like João Vas, Soldado in the Legion of Ponda stated that he did not do so, because he did not take the matter seriously as the revolt in his opinion would be ineffective.[10] Likewise Salvador Alvares da Costa stated that he did not denounce the discussions as he felt that were mere *gallantarias*.[11]

Fr. José Vas stated that he had not denounced the proposed rebellion on the assumption that it was impossible to execute and in fact appeared to be madness.[12]

Others stated that they had delayed in doing so. This is clear from the statement of Francisco Pereira. On August 6, Tenente Gonzaga spoke to him about the proposed revolt and told him that there would be a government run by certain *senhores* (lords/rulers). On hearing this Pereira was disturbed and sought the advice of Chaplain Fr. Francisco José de Jesus Maria whether he should report the matter or not. The priest heard this with a great deal of seriousness and said that they should discuss this in the evening for a final decision. Because of his professional commitment of attending to patients, Pereira could not meet the said priest that evening and decided to report the matter in the morning to the *Marechal de Campo* or to the *Brigadiero*. But before he could do so he learnt that Tenente Gonzaga had been arrested and he kept his denunciation in abeyance.[13]

Back-stabbing

The trial proceedings also disclose that some of the rebels indulged in back-stabbing and double-crossing and that this was done by friends and fellow rebels. The following instances drawn from the trial proceedings prove this.

Tenente Costa and Tenente Toscano had planned to submit a joint denunciation. But as Tenente Toscano was ill, Costa did not wish to wait any longer. He started his moves from July 31, and first made his deposition before Coronel Mira on August 4, 1787. In fact Tenente Toscano in his deposition described Tenente Costa as a person who had done much to make his life a hell.[14]

Fr. Vicente Coutinho had requested Toscano to make his denunciation and that they should do it together but on the same day Fr. Coutinho went alone, and later came to Toscano's house to visit him as he was sick and said in the presence of Sebastião de Noronha "I had gone to make a denunciation and I have mentioned your name in it".[15]

Fr. Pedro Caetano José Lobo stated that on July 18, 1787, after efforts on his part, Fr. Gonsalves and Fr. da Silva appeared to be convinced that they would not go ahead with their plans to stage a revolt. He therefore told Tenente Toscano not to report the issue. The assumption was that as no harm was being done to the *Estado* it was better to remain silent. Later he learnt that the said priests still continued to pursue their plans. Morever Toscano told him on the day of Santiago that he would denounce all that he knew. Therefore Fr. Lobo also decided to denounce before *Arcebispo Primaz* and accordingly he made his denunciation.[16]

Thus we see that Fr. Lobo and Fr. Coutinho, who had at first dissuaded the two Tenentes Toscano and Costa from reporting to the authorities, back-stabbed them, when they made their respective denunciations.

Fr. Monis had overheard a conversation between Fr. Lobo and Fr. Coutinho that they would denounce the proposed revolt. So, he too decided to make his denunciation.[17]

It appears that the three priests Fr. Lobo, Fr. Coutinho and Fr. Monis collectively decided to make their individual denunciations before *Arcebispo Primaz*.

Both Fr. Diogo Benedicto Lobo and the Vicar of Socorro agreed to make a denunciation against the proposed revolt but the Vicar felt sick and returned to his own house. When Fr. Lobo went in search of him to deal with the matter of the denunciation,the Vicar stated that he was feeling better, that after a few days he would return to the church and make the denunciation.

As the Vicar, Fr. Cardozo suddenly turned very ill, was almost dying , Fr. Lobo once again went in search of him. Fr. Cardozo advised him that if there was not enough proof, things could backfire and they would be subjected to punishment. It was for this reason Fr. Lobo did not make his denunciation.[18] Yet strangely and unethically Fr. Cardozo made his denunciation on his death bed.

Another case of double cross and betrayal is narrated below.

Caetano Xavier da Costa of Chicalim, Cabo da Esquadra of the Legion of Ponda, resided in the house of Marechal de Campo, Francisco Antonio da Viega Cabral.

Tenente Gonzaga entrusted Costa with the task of passing on a message to Sebastião de Noronha of Nagoa, that "the *encomenda* was expensive and that he could not buy it". The Cabo was curious about this message and appeared malicious. Therefore Noronha told him about the intended rebellion. He told him that he did not know much, that he (Costa) could investigate and report to Marechal de Campo.[19] According to Caetano Xavier da Costa, Noronha told him that if the matter was reported, the rebels would lose the men that he had arranged for them. Together they decided to deceive the rebels, but meanwhile, unfortunately for them, Sebastião de Noronha was arrested.

In fact, Caetano Xavier da Costa had informed Marechal de Campo that within a short while he would be the bearer of great news. During the trial, Costa said that he wanted to make his denunciation once he received an intimation from Sebastião de Noronha.[20]

This was shocking on the part of Sebastião de Noronha, who was party to the rebellion right from July 1787. Perhaps, fearing that Costa would put him in deep trouble, he took such a stand.

Steps Taken after the Trial

The main trial ended in December 1787, four months after the jury sessions began in August 1787. By a letter dated December 15, 1787 José Joaquim de Sequeira Magalhaens e Lançöes submitted the Report on the *Devassa* relating to those accused of plotting to throw out the Portuguese from Goa and to establish a Republic.[21]

José Joaquim de Sequeira Magalhaens e Lançöes was replaced by José da Rocha Dantas e Mendonça who arrived in the monsoon of 1787 (Sept. 1787). The latter continued with the trial proceedings till January 14, 1788. The examination of some more witnesses remained as he had fallen ill after his arrival.

The trial records along with attachments such as the four letters seized from the *Nau de Viagem* in September 1787, were despatched to Portugal.[22] José da Rocha Dantas e Mendonça submitted the *Devassa* proceedings prepared by Dezembargador José Joaquim de Sequeira Magalhaens e Lançöes.[23]

By *Nossa Senhora da Arrabida* which left the port of Goa on January 20, 1788, the Goa Government sent the first copy

(*1ª via*) of the said *Devassa* proceedings and the second copy (*2ª via*) was sent by *Nau de Viagem Nossa Senhora da Conceição*.[24]

The Goa authorities by their letters dated January 16 and 17, 1788 to Portugal, that indicated the trial was undertaken because of a revolt that some natives intended to carry out to throw the Portuguese out of the *Estado*. The leaders of the *sublevação* were Fr. José Antonio Gonsalves also called José Filipe Gonsalves and Fr. Caetano Francisco de Couto, both natives of the *Estado.* They had gone to Portugal with the intention of being granted bishoprics by Her Majesty. They were denied the same returned to their motherland, in the ship called *Senhor Jesus Resuscitado, Santa Zeferina e Princeza do Brazil*, which left the port of Lisbon in the monsoon of the year 1785, and reached Goa in May 1786. They were filled with anger and indignation, which they demonstrated through their arrogance. They gathered together fellow countrymen of the Brahmin caste and some youth with the goal of instigating a revolt as detailed in the *Devassa* records.[25]

The *Relação* of the accused demonstrated that four priests had escaped and that one of them was none other than Fr. José Antonio Gonsalves, the most active and intelligent of the conspirators and their true leader. He continued to be in hiding.[26]

The said letters of January 1788 give details of the denunciations made on August 5 and 6, 1787 and the efforts made by the Goa authorities to attend to the security of the provinces and the *Estado*, and to deal with enemies who could participate in the *sublevação*.[27]

The said letters also pointed out, that the conspirators in Goa had members and accomplices in Portugal, that this was obvious from the letters that had been seized from the *Nau de Viagem* that arrived from Portugal.[28] The suspected accomplices in Lisbon were José Antonio Pinto and Joaquim Antonio Vicente. *Dezembargador Chancelor de Estado*, José da Rocha Dantas e Mendonça, who had been entrusted with the trial proceedings after the exit of Magalhaens e Lanções had informed that Fr. Caetano Vitorino de Faria was also a suspect.[29]

Therefore all the ships reaching the port of Goa were being checked for information about José Antonio Pinto, Joaquim Antonio, Frade Custodio and Fr. Caetano Vitorino de Faria. The Lisbon authorities were told to take steps to arrest them and that details and necessary clarifications relating to them were being sent with the Capitão of the *Navio*.[30]

As the rebels in Goa had their colleagues in Lisbon, there was the fear that news of the rebellion would leak, if any other ship reached Portugal before the two vessels carrying the *Devassa* records.[31] Therefore orders were issued to the Capitão of the *Navio* that during the voyage to *Reino* to avoid any communication with any ship that could reach the port of Lisbon first, and if it stopped at any of the Islands of Açores, he should present an order, to be opened before the respective Governor or Commandante, so that they should not allow the departure of other vessels, which could take the letters or news about what had occurred in the *Estado da India* to the Lisbon court.[32] On reaching Lisbon, ships coming from Goa had to be searched so that news of the conspiracy did not spread.[33]

Instructions had also been issued to the Governor General of Moçambique to arrest José Antonio Pinto, Joaquim Antonio, Frade Custodio and Fr. Caetano Vitorino de Faria, if they moved to the port of Moçambique in any ship that came from Portugal in the monsoon of 1788.[34]

There was also a request by the Goa authorities for more European troops for the security of the *Estado*.[35]

Difficulties faced by the Government during the Trial.

The *Devassa* faced some delay, because of the replacement of José Joaquim de Sequeira Magalhaens e Lanções, *Chancelor de Estado*, by José da Rocha Dantas e Mendonça, while the trial was going on. Moreover, the latter fell ill on his arrival in Goa.

The indispositions and diseases that the prisoners suffered was another cause of delay .[36] This was not a shocking matter as the prison cells were dark, ill-ventilated and far from hygenic.[37]

After the submission of the *Devassa* records to Lisbon, the Resolution of the Government at Portugal was awaited. The local Government had to use European troops to guard the prisoners as Indian soldiers could not be trusted to keep them safe. With this wait, the security of the *Estado* was at stake.[38] The local authorities were also in a state of confusion about the prisoners mainly the priests, whether they were to be sent to Portugal or to be retained until the Resolution was passed.[39]

Difficulties Prisoners faced

As indicated earlier, the accused were well-guarded by European troops and were initially housed in the Fort of Reys Magos, *Fortaleza de Agoada* and the *Quartel de Pangim*. In the course of time, the jail at the *Casa de Polvora* was used to meet the need to house more prisoners.

Every prisoner was housed in a room, which was very narrow, which was not enough for a *quitanda*. It was dark and badly ventilated and was the root cause of disease. We get a clear idea of the scenario in the jails from a complaint written by Fr. José Manoel de Menezes, a former Vicar of Guirim. He stated that the cell he occupied was such, that besides being dark and dingy he could not speak to anyone, could not pray or read any spiritual material. He was not administered any of the sacraments.[40]

Around October 1788 the prisoners were made to exchange cells and jails. Luis Antonio Gonsalves was moved from *Casa de Polvora* to the Fort of Reys Magos and Sebastião Paula de Noronha from the latter to the former. Likewise Pedro Luis Gonzaga de Souza was shifted from the Fort of Reys Magos to *Casa de Polvora*. Tenente Inacio Toscano exchanged cells with Manoel Luis. The former was taken from Fort of Reys Magos to *Casa de Polvora* and the latter from *Casa de Polvora* to Fort of Reys Magos. Fr. Jorge Dias was shifted from *Casa de Polvora* to the Reys Magos fort. It was a coincidence that Tenente Gonzaga, Tenente Toscano and Sebastião de Noronha, key players in the rebellion were shifted to the *Casa de Polvora*.[41] This re-shuffle took place to counter any leakage of the trial proceedings.

In short the prisoners were treated badly and they underwent much dicomforture. We can even speculate, that night after night, every prisoner lived a life of torment, awaiting his fate and the end of his ordeal.

The *Secretorio de Estado da India* in his letter dated July 21, 1788 to the Governor General of Goa, acknowledged the receipt of the *Devassa* proceedings and ordered that those found guilty should be sentenced.[42]

As indicated earlier, by an order issued on August 9, the Governor General intiated the *Devassa* for the formation of the *prova dos autos* against the criminals jailed in the Fort of Reys Magos, the *Fortaleza de Agoada* and the *Quartel de Pangim*. The Chancellor of the *Relação* recorded the proceedings, statements of the witnesses, interrogations, etc. The process ended in the *Sentença* imposed by the *Relação de Goa* on December 9, 1788, which was sent to Lisbon under cover of the letter of the Governor General dated March 18, 1789.[43] This was accompanied with a judicial copy of the depositions of the witnesses, *testemunhas referidas* and the *Autos*.[44] The *Sentença* did not cover the ecclesiastic prisoners. Punishment was meted out only to the military and the civilians.

Sentença of December 9, 1788 [45]

Death Sentence: Condemned to the Gallows

Tenente Pedro Luis Gonzaga and Tenente Manoel Caetano Pinto of the Legion of Ponda were imposed the highest punishment of all. They were condemned to be bound with ropes, tied to the tails of horses and to the accompaniment of the town crier, they were to be dragged through the streets of the city to the gallows, the place of their execution. Thery were to be allowed to die a natural death. While still alive their hands were to be chopped. After their death, their heads were to be severed from their bodies and fixed to stakes. Their bodies were to be quartered and displayed on high poles in public places in *Isle de Goa* and the provinces of Salcete and Bardez specially in the villages of Candolim and Nerul where they resided and also in the villages of Pilerne, Piedade, Mandur and Nagoa till they decayed with time.

Thirteen others had also to face the death sentence— David Francisco Viegas, Caetano Xavier da Costa, Nicolao Luis da Costa, Inacio Caetano Toscano, Miguel Antonio da Costa, Inacio Caetano Lopes, Salvador Alvares da Costa, Baltazar Caeiro, Manoel Ferrão, Antonio Fernandes, João Vas, José Monteiro and Bernardo de Mesquita. The first two were condemned to be bound with ropes and to the accompaniment of the town crier were to be taken to the gallows and let to die a natural death. While still alive, their hands were to be chopped off. After death their heads were to be severed from their bodies, staked on high poles, and displayed at their place of residence till they decayed with time. In the case of the remaining eleven they were condemned to the gallows. Their heads were to be chopped after death, staked on high poles erected at their places of residence for public display. In addition to this, the assets of all the fifteen, were to be confiscated and their children and grandchildren were to be branded with infamy for all time.

Deportation / Exile

José Luis Guinete of Milan was condemned to be bound with ropes and to the accompaniment of the town crier, he was to be flogged publicly in the streets of the city. He was to be deported for life to serve in the galleys at Angola. Sebastião de Noronha, Cabo at the shore of Bardez, was to be administrated the same punishment mentioned above, except that he was to be deported to Benguela for life. Manoel Luis was to be flogged and condemned to deportation to East Africa, Vicente de Abreu was condemned to be bound with ropes to be flogged in the streets of the city and exiled for ten years to Senna. Francisco Pereira was also imposed the punishment of flogging and ten years of deportation, but to Moçambique.

All those condemned to deportation or exile had also to face the attachment of their assets to the Exchequer and threatened with death, if they tried to return or was seen anywhere in the *Estado*.

Galleys and fines

Lourenço Fernandes was condemned to flogging in the streets and hard labour at the galleys of Goa. Fellipe Fernandes, Vitorino Vas and Vicente Gomes too, had to face the same penalty. All four of them were to be imposed a fine of 100 *xerafins* each as costs for the *Relação*. Micael Silvestre was to be deported to the galleys.

Sebastião Paula de Noronha of Nagoa-Verna died in prison. He was declared a traitor, guilty of high treason, with the brand of infamy on his children. All his assets were attached to the Exchequer and the Royal Council.

Those who were acquitted were as follows:-

(1) João de Souza Onorcar
(2) Fr. Antonio Filipe Vas, Vicar of Moira
(3) Antonio Dias
(4) Manoel Pinto, brother-in-law of Fr. João Baptista Pinto
(5) Narba Naique
(6) Manoel Antonio Gonsalves, brother of Fr. José Antonio Gonsalves
(7) Fr. Sebastião Baptista
(8) Fr. Pedro Dalgado

They were absolved of all charges on grounds that they were innocent or because there was not enough evidence to prove their guilt.

On examining the *Sentença* imposed by the *Relação de Goa* on December 9, 1788, a few comments are in order.

Though the accused got the benefit of a trial it was in all likelihood rigged. It seems strange that Bernardo de Misquita and José Monteiro, both of them were agents / businessmen, faced the death sentence, whereas João de Souza Onorcar who was also an agent, was acquitted. The first two did not deserve such harsh penalty. Manoel Luis, a relative of Fr. Couto faced deportation, whereas Manoel Pinto, brother-in-law of Fr. João Baptista Pinto and Manoel Antonio Gonsalves, brother of Fr. José Antonio Gonsalves escaped punishment. This too is odd.

The *Sentença* imposed on the natives of Goa was extremely harsh. The colonial government looked upon the entire episode of 1787 as *"abominavel delicto de rebellião e alta traição"* (abominable crime of rebellion and high treason) and therefore felt it necessary and apt to mete out such exemplary punishment to send out an ominous signal to the natives, that should remain in their memory for all times.

Cunha Rivara in his work *Conjuração de 1787 em Goa* stated that the rebel priests were not tried. This is not true, specially since their depositions are found in the *Devassa* records and more so since three priests were acquitted – Fr. Antonio Filipe Vas, Fr. Sebastião Baptista and Fr. Pedro Dalgado.

Above all, Cunha Rivara's main arguments in his above mentioned work is conclusively based on the said *Sentença*. But it should be obvious to us that the *Sentença* as well as the work of Cunha Rivara are colonial in nature, defending and justifying the colonial cause.

The Execution

The execution of the fifteen rebels took place on December 13, 1788 in the Campo de Mandovi, *lugar das forças* near the Customs House, in the City of Goa where the gallows were erected.[46]

This public execution was conducted in the most populous part of the city. Gathered there were the nobility, the assistants, officials of the Municipality, the troops and those prisoners who were sentenced to other punishments. They were forced to be present throughout the entire execution till the very end, to witness the spectacle of "*morte natural para sempre*"[47]

The execution of the fifeen natives (few of them had been informers) a symbol of victory for the colonizers, was indeed one of the darkest days in the history of Goa.

The total value of the property that was confiscated from the condemned was 2518 -4-01 *xerafins*.[48]

The value of the assets of some of the condemned may be seen in Table 10.3.

Table 10.3

VALUE OF THE PROPERTY OF SOME OF THE CONDEMNED

Name	Total Value (in *xerafins*)
Caetano Francisco de Couto	63 - 4 - 59
João Baptista Pinto	280 - 3 - 26
Diogo Caetano de Couto	108 - 2 - 54
José Antonio Gonsalves	131 - 1 - 14

Source : HAG: *MR* 174B, fls. 610 - 611

Issue of the Priests

The Goa Government was in a dilemma as to what was needed to be done with the priests implicated in the revolt. Initially there were no instructions from Lisbon. But in July 1788 the Government received orders to dispatch them to Lisbon. Accordingly fourteen priests were sent as prisoners on board the ship *S. Luis e Santa Maria Magdalena*. Antonio Joaquim Reis Portugal, *Capitão* of the said vessel, was handed over the prisoners on March 29, 1789, on the orders of Francisco da Cunha, Governor General of the *Estado da India*. He was to transport them safely and hand them over in Lisbon.[49]

The priests who were sent to Lisbon were:-

1) Caetano Francisco da Silva, Vicar of San Lourenço de Linhares
2) Manoel da Expectação, Vicar of Ponda
3) João Alvares da Souza, Vicar of Pomburpa
4) Miguel Alvares, Vicar of Pilerne
5) Vincente Alvares of Pilerne
6) Caetano Francisco de Couto
7) Mathias Bernardo da Fonseca, Vicar of Chorão
8) Luis Antonio Gonsalves
9) Luis Caetano de Souza

10) José Manoel de Menezes, Vicar of Guirim
11) José Antonio Vas of Anjuna
12) João Baptista Pinto of Candolim
13) Diego Benedicto Lobo of Serula
14) Jorge Dias of Candolim

Of these, thirteen reached Lisbon and one expired on the way. They were immediately taken to the Torre da São Julião da Barra.[50] Fr. Caetano Francisco de Couto behaved differently from the others. He was therefore shifted to the Convent of S. Francisco of the city, to be examined if he was mentally sound. This was reported to the Goa Government by the Secretario do Estado, Martinho de Melo e Castro by letter dated May 9, 1790.[51]

The priests remained in their cells for years together, forgotten, without being produced before a Court. As the confiscated properties of the priests were gradually deteriorating and no action could be taken as the priests had not been imposed any sentence, the Governor of Goa sought a decision from the Lisbon authorities.

In 1802, in pursuance of information received from the Archbishop of Goa, Fr. Manoel da Expectação was declared innocent. The latter was set free and permitted to return to his homeland and reinstated in the service that he had executed prior to his arrest.[52] It was also ordered, that the said priest be paid 400 *reis* per day for life.

Eighteen years had passed since the priests departed from Goa, during which, there were fruitless attempts to obtain their pardon. Eventually the following were sent back to Goa in 1807: Jorge Dias, Caetano Francisco da Silva, Miguel Alvares, Vicente Alvares, Mathias Bernardo da Fonseca, Diogo Benedicto Lobo, João Baptista Pinto and Luis Antonio Gonsalves.[53] All of them were pardoned and their properties duly returned so that they could administer them on their own.[54]

Four of the fourteen priests had passed away, perhaps one on the voyage and three in prison— João Alvares de Souza, José Antonio Vaz, Luis Caetano de Souza and José Manoel de Menezes.

Fr. Inacio Noronha, *Presbiterio Secular*, and his two brothers Remedios de Noronha and Josepha de Noronha who fled to Bombay, were pardoned and permitted to return to Goa.[55] Fr. José Antonio Gonsalves, Fr. Diego Caetano de Couto and Fr. Pedro Fernandes were neither pardoned, nor their properties released.

All the above orders were issued by Viceroy Count of Sarzedas, which he confirmed in his *Officio* dated February 25, 1808.[56]

The priests were not imposed any sentence, even though there was full proof of their guilt. This may be because the clergy had regained their status and powers during the reign of D. Maria, which they had lost earlier. Even though the *Relação de Goa* declared that the case was within the competence of the civilian courts, the court's opinion was not accepted neither was the matter presented before the ecclesiastical court. Perhaps this was out of fear that the priests would be exonerated. So they kept the priests in prison till they died or till the time when they could say that they had atoned enough for their guilt.[57]

The letter of the Secretario de Estado dated May 9, 1790 is the last document that deals with Fr. Francisco Caetano de Couto after he was moved out of the Torre da S. Julião da Barra to be examined for mental illness. There was no news about Fr. Couto after this, or whether he was set free and was in Lisbon, whether he returned to Goa. One version is that he returned to Goa with Fr. Jorge Dias and had moved to South India where he died.[58]

This is the tragic story of the attempted Revolt of 1787 in Goa (commonly known as the Revolt of the Pintos).

Though the rebellion of 1787 never took place, the sentence imposed on the rebels, most of them from Bardez had a strong bearing on the elections of 1861 in Nagoa, Bardez.[59]

Above all, the happenings in Goa in 1787, in all probability impacted the *Mineira Inconfidência* in Brazil, which took place just two years later, which shall be discussed in the next chapter.

REFERENCES

1. AHU: *MI* Maço 155 (153), doc. dtd. 15 Aug. 1787.
2. AHU: *MI* Maço 155 (153), doc. dtd. 15 Aug. 1787.
3. AHU: *MI* Maço 155 (153), doc dtd. 12 Aug. 1787.
4. AHU: *MI* Maço 155 (153), Devassa: *passim.*
5. AHU: *MI* Maço 155 (153), doc dted 10, Dec. 1787.
6. AHU: *MI* Maço 155 (153), Devassa, Auto Nos. 1-46 : *passim.*
7. AHU: *MI* Maço 155 (153), Devassa, Auto Nos. 1-46 : *passim*
8. AHU: *MI* Maço 155 (153), Devassa, Statement of Inacio Caetano Toscano.
9. AHU:*MI* Maço 155 (153), Devassa, Statement of Inacio Caetano Toscano; Auto No. 4, Statement of Fr. Manoel da Expectação.
10. AHU:*MI* Maço 155 (153), Devassa, Auto No. 23, Statement of João Vas.
11. AHU: *MI* Maço 155 (153), Devassa, Auto No. 21, Statement of Salvador Alvares da Costa.
12. AHU: *MI* Maco 155 (153), Devassa, Auto No. 20, Statement of Fr. José Vas.
13. AHU: *MI* Maço 155 (153), Devassa, Auto No.8, Statement of Francisco Pereira.
14. AHU: *MI* Maço 155 (153), Devassa, undtd. Statement of Inacio Caetano Toscano.
15. AHU: *MI* Maço 155 (153), Devassa, Auto No. 6, Statement of Inacio Caetano Toscano.
16. AHU: *MI* Maço 155 (153), Devassa, Auto No. 7, Statement of Pedro Caetano José Lobo.
17. AHU:*MI* Maço 155 (153), Devassa, Witness No. 10, Statement of Inacio Xavier Monis.
18. AHU: *MI* Maço 155 (153), Devassa, Auto No. 36, Statement of Fr. Diogo Benedicto Lobo.
19. AHU: *MI* Maço 155 (153), Devassa, Auto No.29, Statement of Sebastião de Noronha.
20. AHU: *MI* Maço 155 (153), Devassa, Auto No.44, Statement of Caetano Xavier da Costa.
21. AHU: *MI* Maço 155 (153), Devassa, doc. dtd. 15 Dec. 1787.

22. HAG: *MR* 169A, fl. 197v, doc. dtd. 17 Jan. 1788; 170C, fl. 693, doc. dtd. 18 March 1789.
23. HAG: *MR* 169B, fl. 500, doc. dtd. 27 Feb. 1788.
24. HAG: *MR* 169B, fl. 705, doc. dtd. 20 Feb. 1788. AHU: *MI* Maço 155 (153), doc. dtd. 20 Feb.787.
25. AHU: *MI* Maço 155 (153), doc. dtd. 17 Jan. 1788.
26. AHU: *MI* Maço 155 (153), doc. dtd. 17 Jan.1788.
27. AHU: *MI* Maço 155 (153), doc. dtd. 17 Jan.1788.
28. AHU: *MI* Maço 155 (153), doc. dtd. 16 Jan.1788.
29. AHU: *MI* Maço 155 (153), doc. dtd. 16 Jan.1788.
30. AHU: *MI* Maço 155 (153), doc. dtd. 16 Jan.1788.
31. HAG: *MR* 169A, fl. 197v, doc. dtd. 16 Jan. 1788.
32. AHU: *MI* Maço 155 (153), doc. dtd. 20 Feb.1788.
33. HAG: *MR* 169A, fls. 198v-199, doc. dtd. 16 Jan 1788; 169B, fls. 705-706, doc. dtd. 20 Feb. 1788.
34. AHU: *MI* Maço 155 (153), doc. dtd. 16 Jan.1788.
35. AHU: *MI* Maço 155 (153), doc. dtd. 17 Jan.1788.
36. HAG: *MR* 169B, fl. 500, doc. dtd. 26 Feb. 1788.
37. AHU: *MI* Maço 155 (153), Statement of Fr. José Manoel de Menezes.
38. HAG: *MR* 169A, fl. 211, doc. dtd. 17 Jan. 1788.
39. HAG: *MR* 169A, fl. 211, doc. dtd. 17 Jan. 1788.
40. AHU: *MI* Maço 155 (153), Statement of Fr. José Manoel de Menezes.
41. Charles Borges, ed., *Goa and the Revolt of 1787*, p.40.
42. *Loc. cit.*
43. HAG: *MR* 170C, fls. 693-694.
44. HAG: *MR* 170C, fls. 693-694.
45. HAG: *MR* 170A, fl. 23v; 210A; fls. 31v-34v; *Refutção Analytica d'Um Manifesto do Governo Intruz de Goa,* 1835, doc. no. 24.
46. Anita Almeida, pp. 47-83: *passim.*
47. *Loc. cit.*
48. HAG: *MR* 174B, fls. 610-611.
49. HAG: *MR* 170B, fls. 559-560, doc. dtd. 29 March 1789.
50. Borges, *op. cit*, pp. 52-53.
51. *Ibid.*, p. 53.
52. HAG:*MR* 183, fls. 139, 140, 143, *Refutção Analylica*, *op. cit.*, p. 23.
53. HAG: *MR* 186, fls. 286, 290; 187A, fl 287.
54. HAG: *MR* 187A, fls. 286, 287, docs. dtd. 3 Dec 1807, 5 Feb. 1807.
55. HAG: *MR* 187A, fl. 288, doc. dtd. 13 March 1807.
56. Borges, *op. cit.,* p. 55.
57. *Ibid*, p. 56.
58. *Ibid*, p. 62.
59. Mariano Dias "Fr. Caetano Vitorino de Faria" in *Essays in Goan History* ed., T.R. de Souza. p. 141.

11

REVOLTS IN GOA (1787) AND BRAZIL (1789): SIMILARITIES AND DISSIMILARITIES.

News of the aborted uprising in Goa must have reached the shores of far-off Brazil. This is confirmed by a testimony given by a witness during his interrogation, when on trial for the *Inconfidência Mineira* at Brazil. Besides Manuel Inacio Alvarenga, a ringleader of the said *Inconfidencia* was in the know of the tragic history of Fr. José Antonio Gonsalves.[1] Therefore, undoubtedly the most significant impact of Goa's nativist revolt of 1787 was felt in Portugal's Atlantic colony, Brazil.

It would therefore be worthwhile to focus on both the revolts cited above in a comparative framework, as they could easily lend themselves to scrutiny in such a framework. An attempt at comparative analysis, would aim at a better understanding of the specific features of both of them and enable us to situate them within the Portuguese colonial set-up.

Both the above-mentioned episodes of 1787 and 1789 in history lasted for not more than one *semestre*, without combat and bloodshed. Both were attempted revolts, the products of dissatisfaction, profoundly marked, without any doubt, by the tension characteristic in the society of Goa and Brazil in the eighteenth century.

Causes

Intellectualism.

The arms and ammunition of the *Inconfidencia* of Minas Gerais were ideas, books of history and philosophical doctrines of the enlightened. The rebels were exposed to the study of the heroic episodes of the American Revolution of 1776. These ideas and models provided food for nativist sentiments of the *mineiros*, and the people of the other provinces of Brazil, in their movement for emancipation. The revolt of 1787 in Goa, too, had its roots in the ideology of liberty, equality, social justice and republicanism of the American War of Independence. But in the case of Brazil, the issue of enlightenment not only gained ascendancy but went much further. There is overwhelming evidence to show that the political concepts–progressive and liberal–generated an atmosphere in Brazil, in which arose numerous poets, writers of prose, orators, scientists, artists, musicians, etc.–elements that formed, one could consider without any exaggeration, a brilliant mental elite of the country.[2]

The emancipation of the thirteen British colonies of North America and the promulgation of the Constitution of the United States of America in 1776, served as a catalyst for the expansion of the philosophical ideas of liberalism in the Capitannia of Minas Gerais and beyond. Works of Voltaire, Rousseau, Montesquieu, John Locke and Adam Smith had a tremendous impact on the movement. Popular amongst the intellectuals in Vila Rica (Brazil), in the last quarter of the eighteenth century was *História Filsófica e Politica dos Estabelicimentos e do Comercio dos Europeus nas Duas Indias*, a work of Guillaume Thomas Raynal. This work according to Alexandre Miranda Dalgado was particularly appreciated by Brazilian readers as it was the first time that in a book there was information and a critical study on the situation in Brazil and its potentialities.[3]

Recueil des Lois Constitutives des Colonies Anglaises Confédereás sous la Dénomination d'Etats–Unis de L'Amerique Septentrionale was another book that impacted the *Inconfidencia Minerva*. The *Recueil* published in 1778 was dedicated to Benjamin Franklin by Claude Ambrioso Régnier. It became the trademark of the *Inconfidência*. It was translated by José Alvares Maciel, a copy of which was with Tiradentes. Some notes were found written in the margin, on some pages of this copy, which was appended to the *Autos de Devassa*. Both Maciel and Tiradentes were leaders of the movement.

About 1400 volumes were confiscated from the Brazilian rebels. The number of volumes available with some of them were as follows:[4]

Conego Luis Veira da Silva	570
Cláudio Manuel da Costa	389
Fr. Manuel Rodrigues da Costa	200
Fr. Carlos Correia de Teledo	104
Francisco de Paula Freire Andrada	84
José de Resende Costa (father)	60
Inácio José de Alvarenga Peixoto	18

A fermentation of ideas, conspired for Minas Gerais to be a territory that contributed to the formation and consolidation of the aspirations for autonomy. It contributed to the crystallisation of the spirit of emancipation by creating a national conscience, lucid and arrogant. The independence of Brazil owed much to those in Minas Gerais, who by 1788 dreamt of fiscal justice, a University for equality and a Republic.

Portugal, a Fountain of Inspiration.

Necessity can be the mother of glorious invention. As seen earlier, Goans would proceed to Portugal and Italy for further studies. They not only formed a '*Colonia Goesa*' but also came into contact with the ideas of liberalism blowing over Europe. This was a significant cause of the rebellion of 1787. The same can be said of Brazil. Numerous enriched *mineradores* in the Capitannia of Minas Gerais of Brazil would send their sons to European universities, mainly Coimbra and Montpellier. This was at a time when Europe was broadening its intellectual and ideological horizons. They began to articulate like Jefferson, Ambassador of the United States of America in France. José Joaquim da Maia and others dreamt of an emancipated Brazil.[5] José Alvares Maciel, *mineiro* after undergoing a course in Portugal, voyaged to England where he studied science and was a witness to the Industrial Revolution, a basis for a great nation.[6]

These young men born in Brazil on their return to Minas Gerais, brought books and reformist ideas, and above all the ideals of liberalism and republicanism responsible for the evolution of nativist ideas. At first, the conversations at Lisbon and Coimbra were trivial. Later the possibility of a revolution was without doubt presented by the rebel José Alvares Maciel.[7] This idea though part of the Brazilian psyche for centuries, now found reflection and was enriched in the discussions held in Coimbra which became the conscience of the intended uprising in Brazil.[8]

Pombline Era

None can doubt the impact of the Pombaline reforms, in the field of education and intellectualism, on both Goa and Brazil. Learning eventually exposed the natives to concepts of equality, liberalism and nationalism, that eventually gave birth to rebellions both in Goa (1787) and Brazil (1789).

By the *Alvará Régio* of June 28, 1759 Jesuit education was done away with and a *Republica das Letras* was established. The Pombaline reform of *Humanidades* included Latin, Greek, Rhetoric and Poetry, Philosophy, Rationalism and Morality. This impacted both Goa and Brazil. It led to the creation of an *elite letrada ultramarina*.[9]

On March 25, 1760 the *Director Geral* wrote to the Chancelor of *Relação de Goa*, nominating him *commissario na tarefa* for implementing reforms in the *Estado da India*. Before the end of 1760, the *Casa do Chancelor* in Ribandar was conducting examinations and the process for filling up the posts of *Professores* began.[10] The situation was not different in Rio de Janeiro. In the same year, 1760, the *Chancelor de Relação* was appointed *Commisario dos Estudos.* The result was that seventeen *Professores* were selected. This selection was submitted to Portugal for approval. Until 1772 there was much expectation for the creation of an *imposto do subsidio literário*.

But the Lisbon Government went further. With *Carta de Lei* of November 6, 1772, 358 posts of *Professores* of Latin, Greek, Rhetoric and for the first time those for Philosophy, Rationalism and Morality along with 479 posts for *Mestre de Ler, Escrever e Contar* were created. On November 10, 1773 the *Professores* and *Mestres* were officially appointed in their posts. Rio de Janeiro was allotted two posts for *Mestre de Ler*, *Escrever e Contar*, two for *Gramatica Latina*, one for Rhetoric, one for Greek language and for Philosophy, with schools being opened in the beginning of 1774.[11] All this naturally meant, steps against ignorance and fanaticism.

The *Professores* enjoyed the privileges that were provided in the eighteenth century to the nobles and to those occupying civil posts like *Dezembargadores, Magistrados*, *Doutores* etc. Thus Pombaline reforms signified for the first time the professionalism of the function of the *Professor*.[12] The Crown knew that the colonial empire not only required merchants and agriculturists but also intellectuals.

Academia Scientifica of Rio de Janeiro was founded in 1772. There were reunions of botanists, doctors, surgeons, etc. Influenced by José Jacinto Ferreira, it dedicated itself to promoting the knowledge of natural history, chemistry, physics, medicine and agriculture. But one must also remember the *Sociedade Literaria do Rio de Janeiro* founded in 1786. It dedicated itself to natural history, mathematics, medicine and surgery, physics, chemistry, general and special history, geography and *belas artes*.[13]

To sum up, the Pombaline era had indeed initiated far-reaching changes in Portugal's overseas world. However with the death of D. José I and the establishment of the government of D. Maria I, one saw the return of fanaticism, hypocrisy and superstition.

Socio-Economic conditions.

Society in Brazil was open but not democratic. It was stratified. There was the dichotomy of master and slave. This social divide was responsible for an atmosphere in the cities for the liberty of man.[14] In Goa, the main problem was colour bar–the whites versus the natives. Goan society was also caste-based, specially with the pre-dominance of the Brahmins. Social conditions therefore appeared to be similar in both Brazil and Goa. But Brazil also had significant economic reasons for the revolt of 1789. There was a crisis particularly with respect to mining. Riches, due to gold was illusive.[15] The imposition of the *derrama* almost made the Brazilian economy get into a tailspin.

Rulers and Administrators.

The Portuguese administration was weak and unstable and its machinery, vague and unclear. It was aggravating, with a climate of discontent prevailing in both Goa and Brazil. Colonial power rested on the application of coercive force. Brazil in particular, was scathing with resentment, with the prospect of payment of *derrama* to clear an enormous debt of about 550 *arrobas* of gold to Portugal.[16]

Queen D. Maria I was conscious of the harsh fiscal and judicial measures decreed in the *Cartas Régias* that were directed against Portugal's overseas possessions. She was quick to sign the documents presented to her by her Ministers. Much responsibility for the situation should also be placed on the Secretario, Martinho de Melo e Castro, who chose the Viceroys, Governors of the Capitannias of Brazil, Magistrates etc. To him one could also attribute the execution of the *ordens régias*.

The communication between the *Corte* and the *Ultramar* was full of misgivings. Above all, it was always slow and incomplete, when not infected with the vice of corruption. Martinho de Melo e Castro was well-experienced in diplomatic functions and understood profoundly all overseas matters. There was no information or intrigue that escaped his attention or which he did not record.[17] But he had a touch of arrogance as indicated by Fr. Gonsalves in the *praticas* held in Goa. This was evident in the audiences that Fr. Caetano Vitorino de Faria had with him in Lisbon. The attitude of the Lisbon Government was echoed by the local authorities. Governors, Luis da Cunha Menezes and Visconde de Barbacena in Brazil were not unlike their counterparts who governed colonial Goa.

The corruption prevailing amongst the administrators in the colonies was well-known. Barbacena came to govern Minas Gerais at a time when he was in a state of debt in Lisbon, but returned to the Metropolis rich. In Minas Gerais there was visible expression of the nature of colonial administration in literature and art. The satire of Francisco Melo Franco and Tomaz Antonio Gonzaga, the epic of Basilio da Gama, the lyric of Claudio Manuel da Costa and the work of Alvarenga Peixoto amongst others, were significant. There were also strong manifestations in sculpture, architecture and even painting. Native art by Antonio Francisco Lisboa is notable.[18] Such manifestations were not visible in Goa.

The Rebels

In Goa, with the exception of one from Italy, all the rebels were natives – a motley mixture of the clergy, military and civilians, largely belonging to the Brahmin caste and mainly from Ilhas, Bardez and Salcette. In Brazil, we see the presence of the *mineiros* of the numerous towns of Minas Gerais, and from other regions, amongst whom were the rich and the influential. The richest of them was Alvarenga Peixoto. According to Kenneth Maxwell, the conspiracy of *mineiros* was basically a movement of the oligarchy and was in the interest of the oligarchy though proclaimed in the name of the masses.[19] The *mineiros* not only included whites but also *mazombas, negros* and *mulatos*. They associated themselves with *cariocas* like Inacio José de Alvarenga Peixoto, Francisco de Paula Freire de Andrada and the *fluminense* Salvador Carvalho do Amaral Gurgel. They obtained the support of some opulent persons of São Paulo, of *paulistas* Carlos Correa de Teledo and his brother Luis Vas, and of Capitão Rego Fortes of the *Legião dos Voluntarios Reais de São Paulo*. Gonzaga of Porto had an origin that was *pernambucana* and half *carioca*. Domingos de Abreu Viera, Vicente Viera da Mota and Antonio de Oliveira Lopes were Portuguese. Curiously there was the involvement of an Irish, Nicolau Jorge Gwerck.[20]

The *Inconfidência Mineira* had succeeded in gathering people from all walks of life, men of letters and proletarians, the whites and the blacks, the *reinois* and the *mulatos*, the rich and the not so rich, the urban and the rural, functionaries, owners of plantations, businessmen, mine-owners, doctors, advocates, clergy, money-lenders, poets, skilled workmen, artisans–a collection of spirits and sentiments cemented by the aspiration of liberty and progress.[21] But one cannot deny the fact, that while, some aimed at the movement for autonomy and independence, others had vested interests, not unlike the situation with respect to the *sublevação de Goa* of 1787.

Undoubtedly the ringleader of the *Inconfidência Mineira* was the simple *alferes,* Tiradentes, whose name was actually Joaquim José da Silva Xavier, was born in a family of seven children. Two of his brothers were clerics and one was *capitão das milicias*.[22] Tiradentes was entrusted with the official work of curbing contraband. He moved between Vila Rica and Rio de Janeiro guarding the roads. This involved constant travel, which made him a popular figure.[23] This in turn helped the cause he was espousing.

Fr. José Antonio Gonsalves at Goa, too travelled excessively in 1787, not for ecclesiastic work, but from church to church, from one *assemblea* to another, in order to instigate the clergy to rise against the Portuguese rule. He also did his best to gather funds and support from the natives serving in the army. He emerged as the foremost leader of the revolt of 1787 in Goa.

However Fr. Gonsalves was dissimilar to Tiradentes with regard to the fact that when the revolt was discovered, he managed to escape arrest and punishment. Tiradentes on the other hand boldly and valiantly took full responsibility for his role in the *Inconfidencia Minerva* and faced beheading, loss of property and disgrace for himself and his family.

Like in Goa, the rebels in Brazil would meet and hold discussions (*praticas*) to gather support and assistance, and to draw up plans. One can affirm with all certainty that July 23, 1788 marked the day of the first meeting held at Rio de Janeiro in the house of a businessman José Freire.[24] In a hopeful, animated and enthusiastic discussion amongst three Brazilians – Maciel of Vila Rica, Rolim of Tejuco and Tiradentes of São José del-Rei, the *Inconfidência Mineira* was born. The three *mineiros* were filled with pride for their native land and dreamt of its political emancipation.[25] It needs to be emphasized that, likewise, liberation was the only goal of the unsuccessful revolt of 1787 in Goa.

Meetings were held by the Brazalian rebels from time to time at different places (even in rented premises) with different people. The rebels at these meetings might have stressed on liberty and the establishment of the Republic, but without realistic sights, lacking in objectivity and viability. Their thoughts were more on regional lines and less on the national.[26]

The month of October 1788 was truly important in the history of the conspiracy in Brazil. All the main personalities in the drama were in Minas Gerais–Fr. Rolim, Maciel, Gonzaga, Vicar of São José, Tiradentes, Francisco de Paula Freire da Andrada, Domingos Vidal de Barboza and Silva Alvarenga. A reunion was held in São José on October 9–an *assembeia* for liberty not unlike that in Goa.[27]

The movement for freedom in Brazil in 1789, was mainly restricted to Minas Gerais – Vila Rica, São João del– Rei, São José del– Rei, Sabara and other places.[28] In Goa too, the proposed revolt engulfed only Ilhas, Bardez and Salcette. Other parts of the *Estado da India* remained indifferent.

Future Government

Just like in Goa, the *mineiros* opted for a Republic, but they had arrived at much more detailed and concrete plans, based on which their future government would rest. Certain features stand out in clear relief. They are as follows:[29]

(1) The establishment of the United States of Brazil, having three supreme powers–a bicameral Legislature, an Executive and a Judiciary. Though independent, they would work in harmony.

(2) The Government would draw its authority from popular assent exercised through an electoral system.

(3) The Republic would be divided into Provinces. Each Province would have its own Municipality empowered to legislate on provincial matters. The Provinces would be sub-divided into other administrative units.

(4) The Executive powers were to be exercised by a President, elected by a system of universal suffrage. The Provinces were to be headed by Governors and the Municipal units by *Prefeitos*. For the President, and all others cited above, general elections were to be held every three or four years. The President could be re-elected. The *Camaras Municipais* would be composed of *vereadores*, the number of which would be proportionate to the population they represented.

(5) The Legislature would be competent to make laws and elaborate them. It would elect the members of the *Camara* and the *Senado Confederais*, the *Camaras Provinciaes* and the *Camaras Municipais*.

(6) To safeguard the national independence and for the maintenance of law and order a permanent milicia would be set up.

(7) All those born in Brazil, whether free or enslaved, would be Brazilian citizens.

(8) All the Brazilian citizens and even resident foreignors were to be equal before the law.

(9) The Republic was to be symbolized by a flag, depicting an equilateral triangle, on the three sides of which, would figure the words “Libertas Quae Sera Tamen”.

(10) Vila of São João del-Rei would be the capital of the Province of Minas Gerais.

Transitory Provisions

(1) Everyone would be free to dress as they wished. They would abolish the provision that prevented the plebians from the use of satin clothes.
(2) Diamonds would be exempted from taxation.
(3) The Government would assure the total liberty of commerce.
(4) There would be freedom to work.
(5) The Republic would promote popular culture through schools, libraries and the press.
(6) The University would be the nucleus for the diffusion of education.
(7) The Republic would promote the economic value of the mineral reserves, and manufactures.
(8) The focus would be on industrialization (iron and textiles) with the development of mineral exploration.
(9) The autonomy of the local market, *vis-à-vis* the foreign, would be established.
(10) The Republic would create a system of incentives for large families so as to increase the population.
(11) The Legislature would be competent to amend the Constitution.

The above plans, for a future government, evidently indicates that all the sections of Brazilian society were attended to. The rebels could ill-afford to alienate the humbler members of society, belonging to different economic strata.

Plan of Action

The rebels of Brazil drew up their *modus operandi* for the revolt:[30]

- Protest against *derrama*.
- Shout at night in Vila Rica "Long live Liberty".
- People were required to run to the square.
- Francisco de Paula had to form an army under his command.

- In Cachoeira do Campo, the Governor Visconde de Barbacona was to be beheaded and his head was to be brought to Vila Rica, or the Governor and his family were to be transported beyond the limits of the Capitannia.
- If the head of the Governor was brought to Vila Rica, the people were required to clamour for the Republic.
- Kill all those who opposed the rebellion.
- The *Fazenda Real* was required to write off the debts of all.
- All the funds in the public treasury would be seized and used to pay the army.
- The capital would be shifted to São Paulo del Rei.
- To establish a university in Vila Rica.
- To be free of taxation on gold and diamonds.
- To promulgate the laws for the government of the New Republic.
- To have a popular force (army) to defend the New Republic.

The rebels of Minas Gerais were seriously disorganized. The original plan was modified several times, before Governor Barbacena discovered the conspiracy on March 15, 1789.[31] Above all, there was no proper plan of action for D-Day as in the case of Goa, and therefore the rebels in Minas Gerais appeared ill-prepared for the venture. In Goa there was a three-pronged approach, much more detailed, focused and viable. Moreover, the day scheduled for the revolt was fixed i.e. before the arrival of the *Nau de Viagem* in September, 1787.

Denunciations

The near idyllic picture in Brazil was flawed when denunciations began.

The Governor of Minas Gerais Visconde de Barbacena, in the beginning of March suspended the *derrama*, when news reached him of a popular uprising in gestation. The rumours were confirmed by the denunciation of Joaquim Silveiro dos Reis.[32]

Denunciations made in Brazil in 1789 were similar to those done in Goa in 1787.

Joaquim Silveiro decided to seize the advantage of getting into the good books of the authorities and of acquiring *beneficios* for himself. He first made his denunciation verbally to Barbacena on March 15, 1789. This was like the verbal denunciation of Tenente Inacio Toscano in Goa. Governor Barbacena wanted Silveiro to put down his denunciation in writing. The first written denunciation against the *Inconfidência Mineira* was made on April 11, 1789 and was personally handed over to the Governor four days later.[33]

The second denunciation was initiated by Basilio de Brito Malheiro do Lago, a native of Ponte de Lima. His denunciation too was initially verbal. This was followed by a long letter dated April 15, 1789 full of names and more detailed than that of Joaquim Silveiro. The third letter of denunciation was written by Inacio Correa Pamplona. A letter dated April 20 was received by Barbacena on May 5. Pamplona revealed that the Vicar of São José informed him of the proposed project implicating its principal articulators Tiradentes and Gonzaga.[34]

When this was followed by repression and arrest, the denunciations multiplied. There were innumerable *denuncias* made by the conspirators themselves—Francisco de Paula Friere de Andrada, Francisco Antonio de Oliveira Lopes, Domingos de Abreu Viera, José de Resende Costa father and son and Domingos Vidal de Barboza.[35]

The denunciations made in Brazil are reminiscent of those that were made in Goa. Sheer spite, the need to save one's skin and personal gain were at the root of these denunciations.

Immediate Official Response and Trial

The Governor of the Capitannia of Minas Gerais informed the Viceroy on March 25, 1789 about the intended revolt. On May 10, 1789 on the orders of Tenente Francisco Vidigal, the house at Rua dos Latoeiras was encircled by patrols of the *Regimento de Extremoz* and Tiradentes was arrested.[36] Other arrests followed. The prisoners were housed in the Fortaleza da Ilha das Cobras. Here till the end of the trial were Vicar Toledo and his brother Luis, Alvarenga, Gonzaga, Conego Luis Viera, Domingos de Abreu Viera, Alferes Ferreira, Coronel Oliveira Lopes, Freire da Andrada, Tiradentes, José Alvares Maciel and others "*seguros e incomunicaveis*".[37]

As in Goa, the Brazilian jails that housed the accused were dark, dingy and ill-ventilated. The trial started at Rio de Janeiro on May 7, 1789. Eleven witnesses were examined upto June 8, 1789. It appears that a second and separate trial was conducted at Vila Rica from June 12, 1789.[38]

The prisoners faced the torture of a long trial i.e. three years from May 7, 1789 to April 18, 1792.[39] This was unlike the trial in Goa, which lasted about six months. Tiradentes, for instance, was interrogated thrice in May 1789. His interrogation resumed after eight months in 1790, first on January 18 and next on February, 4. There was a further interruption of 14 months and the enquiries resumed on April 11, 1791. In June 1791 he was interrogated again.[40] The prisoners remained incarcerated in the said Fortaleza at Rio awaiting their fate. Though the judicial proceedings of the *Inconfidência* was delayed for three years, it was simultaneously and permanently accompanied by public opinion with sincerity, devotion and interest.

As in the case of Goa, the *Inconfidência Mineira* was proclaimed as a crime of "*Lesa Majestade de Primeira Cabeça*".[41] A crime of *Lesa Majestade* could not be extinguished, and disgrace and infamy was even branded on sons and grandsons of the criminals. Property was confiscated in favour of the Crown. Those who had acquaintance with the criminals and knew of their seditious plans but consented to keep silent, would also be treated as criminals and charged with the same crime and had to be subjected to the same punishment.

Depositions made during the trial at Brazil could be summarized as follows:-[42]

(a) nativist sentiments for the establishment of a Republic.

(b) collective enthusiasm for independence, on the lines of British America leading to the formation of the United States of North America.

(c) leadership of Tiradentes and other intellectuals Tomas Antonio Gonzaga and Claudio Manuel da Costa and priests José Oliveira Rolim and Luis Viera da Silva.

(d) revolt against excessive taxation, without any concession of the right to political representation.

(e) revolt against the intentions of the Crown to win over the troops with offers and deception.

(f) need to shift of the capital from Minas Gerais to São João del – Rei.

(g) need for the establishment of institutions of higher education in Minas Gerais for the study of laws like that in Coimbra.

Sentence

Condemned to Death

On Tiradentes was imposed the death sentence. He had to be led through public streets to the *lugar da força*. He had to be beheaded and his head would be taken to Vila Rica. It was to be fixed on a high stake and kept on display at a public place, till it decayed. His body had to be quartered and fixed to stakes and kept on display at populated areas at the site of Varginha and das Sebola, where he had his notorious discussions (*praticas*).

Disgrace was to be imposed on him, his sons and grandsons. His property was to be attached to the *Fisco* and *Camara Real*. The house where he lived was to be demolished and the area salted (*salgada*) so that never more on this land anything could be built. The land was to be evaluated and accordingly the landlord would be paid for the property which would be confiscated. On the same ground a standard would be raised to conserve the memory of this abominable criminal.[43]

There were others who were sentenced to death, which strangely was later commuted to exile to different parts of Africa.[44] Maciel was condemned to death but this penalty was reduced to exile in Angola where he died in 1804.[45] Inacio José de Alvarenga Peixoto also considered to be the leader and head of the conspiracy was imposed the death sentence. He was to be beheaded. His head was to be displayed publicly near his house in São João del – Rei. His property was to be attached to *Camara Real*. Infamy was proclaimed for him and his family. However, his sentence was reduced to exile at Ambaca, 220 kms from Luanda, where he died in 1793.[46]

The others on whom the death sentence was imposed were:-[47]

(1) Francisco de Paula Freire de Andrada
(2) Domingos de Abreu Viera.
(3) Claudio Manuel da Costa
(4) Luis Vas de Toledo
(5) Francisco Antonio de Oliveira Lopes
(6) Domingos Vidal de Barbosa
(7) José de Resende Costa (father and son).
(8) Salvador Carvalho do Amaral Gurgel.

Of the nine above, Claudio Manuel da Costa died on July 4, 1789 under mysterious circumstances. Whether it was suicide or assassination is not known. But for the rest their death sentence was reduced. (Table 11.1)

Table 11.1

REDUCTION IN DEATH SENTENCE (*INCONFIDÊNCIA MINEIRA*)

Name of the Criminal	Reduction/Commutation of Death Sentence	Remarks
Francisco de Paula Freire de Andrada	Perpetual exile to Pedra de Angoche (Moçambique)	He returned to Brazil in 1808.
Luis Vaz de Toledo	Perpetual exile to Angola	Died in 1804
Domingos de Abreu Vieira	Perpetual exile to Ambaca, Angola	Died in Ambaca, Angola in the 1790s.
Francisco Antonio de Oliveira Lopes	Perpetual exile to Benguela	
Domingos Vidal de Barbosa	Exile to Ilha de São Tiago	He was incarcerated in the Convento de São Francisco till his death in 1793.
Resende Costa (father and son)	Exile 1. For father to Bissau. 2. For son to Cabo Verde	Father died in Bissau in 1841; son returned to Brazil in 1804 and was elected in 1821 *Deputado às Cortes*.
Salvador Carvalho do Amaral Gurgel	Exile in Moçambique	He was denied entry in Brazil. He served as *Presidencia de Camara* in Inhambane where he died in 1813

Source : Donatello, Grieco, pp. 110 – 133 : *passim*.

Exile

Vitorino Gonsalves Veloso was imposed the penalty, of first being led into the public streets, then being whipped, followed by perpetual exile at Angola including confiscation of half of his property.[48] Others who were subjected to exile may be seen in Table 11.2.

Table 11.2

SENTENCE OF EXILE (*INCONFIDÊNCIA MINEIRA*)

Name	Nature of Exile	Remarks
Tomas Antonio Gonzaga	Perpetual exile in Angola	He moved from Angola to Moçambique. He died there in 1810
João da Costa Rodrigues	Perpetual exile in Novo Redondo, Benguela	
Antonio de Oliveira Lopes	Exile in Macúa Moçambique for 10 years	He died in exile
João Dias da Mota	Exile of 10 years in Benguela	
Vicente Vieira da Mota	Perpetual exile in Angola	
José Aires Gomes	Exile in Moçambique	He died in exile.

Source: Donatello, Grieco, pp. 138-152

Fernando José Ribeiro and José Martins Borges were punished for false denunciation against Capitão João de Almeida e Souza. Both of them were imposed different penalties.[49] Ribeiro was imposed the penalty of perpetual exile to Benguela and a fine of 200$000 towards the expenses of the *Relação*. Borges was condemned to whipping in the public roads and ten years at the galleys (*de gales*) or hard labour at the works of the *Estado*.[50]

Four persons were absolved of guilt, namely, Faustino Soares de Araujo, João Francisco das Chagas, Alexandre and Manuel da Costa Capanema. Manuel Joaquim de Sá Pinto do Rego Fortes and Francisco José de Melo died in prison.[51]

There were others who had been arrested and released perhaps due to lack of evidence or because they were rich and influential or because they were able to wheedle out of a penalty. Nicolau Jorge Gwerck, José de Sá Bittencourt, João Rodrigues de Macedo, João de Araujo e Oliveira, Joaquim Antonio Gonzaga, Diogo Pereira de Vasconcelos and Joaquim Ferreira dos Santos had been arrested and later released. Claro José e Toledo had disappeared.[52]

Five priests were tried and as per the *Acordão*, two of them were condemned to death namely Fr. Carlos Correia de Toledo e Melo and Fr. José da Silva e Oliveira Rolim. But meanwhile, as per *Carta Regia* of October 15, 1790 the priestly prisoners were transferred to Lisbon to await their fate. The former left for Lisbon where he was incarcerated in a convent where he died in 1800. The latter secretly left for Lisbon towards the end of June 1792. He was initially placed in the Forte de São Julião da Barra. After six years he was moved to the Convento de São Bento da Saude. He was freed in 1803 and allowed to return to Brazil where he died at the age of 88.[53]

Fr. José Lopes de Oliveira for being a "*sabedor e consentidor*" was moved to Lisbon where he was incarcerated in São Julião da Barra and in this fort he died in 1796.

Conego Luis Viera da Silva had been sentenced to perpetual exile in Ilha de São Tome and loss of property. He was initially however, housed in the Fortaleza de São Julião da Barra at Lisbon and later shifted to the Convento de São Francisco in the city. He returned to Brazil and died in 1809.[54]

Fr. Manuel Rodrigues da Costa had been condemned to perpetual exile in Ilha do Principe and loss of property. This priest left for Lisbon and was for four years in the Fortaleza de São Julião da Barra and in the Convento de São Francisco. He was freed in 1804 and returned to Brazil. He was elected in 1821 as *Deputado às Cortes* and eventually died in 1844.[55]

Execution

On April 21, 1792 the city of Rio de Janeiro was a witness to a public spectacle, the execution of Tiradentes. He was the only one who ultimately faced the death sentence.

A glittering military procession in the streets led Tiradentes to the gallows fixed at a public square, Largo da Lampadosa in the vicinity of the city. Around 11 o'clock in the morning, after speeches and acclamations in praise of the Queen, before a silent multitude, the sentence of Tiradentes was carried out. He was beheaded and his body quartered. This dark event–the last few moments in the life of Tiradentes—left an indelible image on the minds of the Brazilians.

The death of Tiradentes was celebrated by the authorities. For three consecutive days there was public illumination and on April 26, the *Te Deum* was sung in the Church of Terceiros do Carmo, as an act of thanksgiving to the Almighty for having helped uncover the conspiracy. In the Church more than 200 candles were lit. This was organized by Viceroy D. José de Castro to serve as a example '*ilesa do contagio de tão infame conspiração*".[56]

The head of Tiradentes was taken in a *bolsa de couro(leather bag)* full of salt, to Vila Rica and fixed to a tall stake and was on public display at a spot that was on the border of Paço and Cadeia. However the head was not displayed for more than one day. In an act of compassion, it was removed from the stake and buried in what later came to be regarded as sacred land.

The four quarters of the decapitated body were transported to Barbacena, Queluz, Varginha do Lourenço and Sebolas. The mortal remains were then taken to Sebolas and buried there. Today a chapel stands on that spot. The bones and other relics of the *Inconfidencia* are at the Museu Sacra Histórico, in the Third District of Paraiba do Sul which today is called Promártir.

In accordance with the sentence imposed the house of Tiradentes was razed to the ground and the land salted. An infamy standard was raised there. This standard was demolished on September 21, 1821 by an order of the Provisional Government of the Capitannia of Minas Gerais.[57] Tiradentes was bestowed the titles of "*Patrono Civico da Nação Brasileira*", "*Protomartir da Inconfidência*" and "*maior brasileiro da todos os tempos*".[58] He was venerated as a martyr. Though the house at Vila Rica was destroyed, in its place, all over Brazil arose roads, avenues, squares, etc. dedicated to Tiradentes. The man condemned by the colonial government as the leader of the conspiracy of 1789, was lionized as a bonafide national hero. He had travelled along the path that elevated him into Brazilian nationalism.

A similar spectacle of a public execution was carried out in Goa more than three years earlier (December 13, 1788). It was not one person but fifteen persons who faced this. Charles Boxer has indicated that this discrimination was based on the Portuguese policy of colour bar. In the case of Brazil, those condemned to death were whites but in the case of Goa all of them were natives (coloured).[59]

Impact

The impact of the *Inconfidência Mineira* though doomed, captured the imagination of the people of Brazil. It floated into music, art, architecture and literature. But the most obvious work was the monument that immortalized the martyr Tiradentes, erected on the spot where his head was on public display, in the centre of the square in the city of Ouro Prato. The square got the name of Praça Tiradentes.[60] In Goa, no monument has been raised in honour of the fifteen martyrs of 1787, not even a square or a street is named after them.

There were several artists who produced paintings, sculptures, pieces of music, etc on Tiradentes. The latter even figured on stamps and currency.[61]

In conclusion it must be said that it is evident to all that there is much in common and much connection between the two rebellions under discussion. The said rebellions had different starting points (place and time) but had the same historical context and was planned and ended in a near identical manner.

REFERENCES

1. Anita Correa Lima de Almeida, "Goa de 1787 e Rio de Janeiro de 1794: Inconfidencia no Imperio", pp. 82-83.
2. Donatello Grieco, *Historia Sincera da Inconfidência Mineira*, Rio de Janeiro, 1990, p. 30.
3. *Ibid.*, pp. 30-33.
4. *Ibid.*, pp. 33-36.
5. Francisco Iglesias "O Clima Politico e a Articulação da Inconfidencia", *Cultura: O Estado de S. Paulo*, Ano VII, no. 456, pp. 2-3.
6. *Ibid.*, p.3.
7. Carlos Guilherme Mota, "Dos Discursos Sedição", *Cultura: O Estado de S. Paulo*, Ano VII, no. 456, p.6.
8. *Loc. cit.*
9. Almeida, *op. cit.* pp.47-83.
10. *Loc. cit.*
11. *Loc. cit.*
12. *Loc. cit.*
13. *Loc. cit.*
14. Iglesias, *op. cit.*, p.2.
15. *Loc. cit.*
16. *Loc. cit.*
17. Grieco, pp. 74-75.
18. Iglesias, *op. cit.*, p.2.
19. Kenneth Maxwell, *Conflicts and Conspiracies. Brazil and Portugal, 1750 – 1808* in Grieco, *op. cit.*, p.12.
20. Grieco, *op. cit.*, pp.28-29.
21. *Ibid.*, p.29.
22. Helio Demante, "Tiradentes, Mito da Nacionalidade", *Cultura : O Estado de S. Paulo*, Ano VII, no. 456, p.10.
23. *Loc. cit.*
24. Grieco, *op. cit.*, p. 56.
25. *Loc. cit.*
26. Iglesias, *op. cit*, p.3.
27. Grieco, *op. cit.* p.57.
28. *Ibid.*, p.62.
29. *Ibid.*, pp.43-45; Iglesias, *op. cit.* p.3..
30. Grieco, *op. cit.* pp. 91-92; Iglesias, *op. cit.*, p.3.
31. Grieco, *op. cit.*p.13.
32. *Ibid.*, p.21.
33. *Ibid.*, p.50.
34. *Ibid.*, pp.51-52.
35. Iglesias, *op.cit.*, p.3.
36. Grieco, *op.cit.*, p.59.
37. *Ibid.*, p. 63.
38. *Ibid.*, pp.60-61.
39. *Ibid.*, p. 11.

40. *Ibid.*, pp.86-87.
41. *Ibid.*, pp.27, 91.
42. *Ibid.*, pp.61-62.
43. *Ibid.*, pp.92-93.
44. *Ibid.*, p. 95.
45. *Ibid.*, p. 56.
46. *Ibid.*, p. 108.
47. *Ibid.*, pp.110-133: *passim.*
48. *Ibid.*, p. 141.
49. *Ibid.*, p. 153.
50. *Loc. cit.*
51. *Ibid.*, pp.176-180.
52. *Ibid.*, pp.180-183.
53. *Ibid.*, pp.157-164.
54. *Ibid.*, pp.165-169.
55. *Ibid.*, pp.170-171.
56. *Ibid.*, pp.96-97; Almeida , *op.cit.*, pp. 47-83.
57. Grieco, *op.cit.* pp. 98-99.
58. *Ibid.*, p. 100.
59. Charles Boxer, *The Portuguese Seaborne Empire*, London, 1969, pp. 199-200.
60. Christina Avila, "Ambiência Artistica e Produção Iconográfica", *Cultura: O Estado de S. Paulo*, Ano VII, no. 456, pp. 8-9.
61. *Ibid.*, pp.8-10: *passim.*

12

CONCLUSION

The conclusions arrived at in this chapter, have their source in the depositions made by the witnesses and the accused during the trial.

One can easily conclude that the episode of 1787 in Goa was not just a protest, or a resistance or a campaign or a public manifestation against the Portuguese government. It was pure and simple, a revolt or a rebellion of the natives to end the rule of the Portuguese in Goa, to liberate it and to establish a Republic–a government of their own.

The fountain of inspiration was the American War of Independence and the winds of change–liberalism, social justice and republicanism–blowing over Europe and the rest of the world, which emboldened a group of Goans to hatch a plot to raise the banner of revolt. Nativist sentiments were for liberation and the establishment of a Republic.

The leadership of the revolt of 1787 remained with the clergy, but the participation was more broad-based in which the number of non-clerics surpassed that of the clerics. Not only the clergy but also the military and civilians dared to plan and execute the revolt. Though the clergy took great pride in their leadership (deposition of Fr. Couto), it was the military and the civilians that faced the brunt of barbaric punishment, ranging from death sentence and banishment to hard labour at the galleys.

Some historians have dismissed the episode of 1787 as one launched by Fr. José Gonsalves and Fr. Caetano Francisco de Couto because of their vested interests – the denial of bishoprics in India. But can one ignore and deny that the exclusion of the natives from high-ranking posts is not an issue of absence of equality and social justice? History has revealed that movements in the world (including those in Goa and the rest of India) had issues, on their agenda, which one could term as 'vested interests' or 'grievances'. The Rebellion of 1857 in India is a case in point. Therefore, it is totally unfair and wrong to dismiss the happenings of 1787 in Goa as just a movement, initiated by some disgruntled clerics, for personal interest and not for equality, social justice, and freedom. The matter of the denial of promotion to Fr. Gonsalves and Fr. Couto was not the only cause of the revolt of 1787, it was only the immediate cause that had added fuel to the burning fire. If we do not accept this, how do we justify the happenings of 1857 in India and consider it a revolt or even a War of Independence? Was the greasing of the cartridges with animal fat that disturbed nativist feelings and sentiments, the only cause for the rise of some sections of India against the British rule or were there other causes arising from 'grievances'?

Some writers have even questioned whether the plotting for the revolt ever took place. This needs to be refuted. The evidence available in the *Devassa* records is an answer to all attempts to belittle the revolt. Secondly, why did the authorities take the happenings of 1787 so seriously so as to impose such severe sentences on the rebels? The history of Goa is dotted with protests, resistances, revolts, mutinies, etc. Have we any evidence of such harsh punishments of death meted out, in each of these cases? This is because the Portuguese were convinced that there was much substance in the events of 1787. The rebels took the task of expelling the Portuguese from India seriously, the Portuguese in turn looked at the matter seriously and eventually dealt with the rebels in an extremely serious manner, with the public execution of fifteen persons.

Nonetheless, it would be wrong to deny that the movement did not suffer from limitations.

The movement of 1787 in Goa was brief and unsuccessful. It never got off the ground. It ended without a single shot. Just as remarkable as the boldness of the attempted revolt, is the speed by which it came to an end.

It was not a national affair. It was confined to Ilhas, Bardez and Salcette and that too in only pockets of them. It did not engulf the rest of the *Estado da India*. Except for Ponda, the New Conquest areas remained aloof.

From the depositions in the *Devassa* records, it is clear that the movement of 1787 was a movement for freedom and the establishment of a Republic, but from it we get no details of the nature of the Republic or of the future government. In this respect the plans of the rebels were indeed vague.

The participation in the said revolt was one-sided and lacked cohesion. It included Christians largely of Brahmin origin. Hindus, Muslims and others in Goa were either excluded or remained indifferent.

Documentation on the trial proceedings, tell us that the plan of action for D-Day–the role of the army specially the Legions of Ponda and Bardez, that of the Vicars in their respective parishes, plans to poison the bread to be administered to the Portuguese soldiers and to render them senseless for a few days with a special drink–was indeed detailed and appeared to be appropriate. But what was really required was loyalty and a united front of all the natives in the armed forces, and the people of Goa, irrespective of caste and creed. It needs to be emphasized here that it was such a lack of unity that was one of the main reasons for the failure of the Uprising of 1857 in India.

The rebels often spoke of foreign assistance to their cause, whether of Germany, Tipu Sultan of Mysore, Bhonsles, Marathas, Sunda King, ruler of Travancore, etc. This is evident from the depositions made by witnesses and the accused. There appears to be little or no truth in all this. Several studies substantiate this statement. If it had been so, there would have been more details about the same in the conspiracy plans. There are also contradictions relating to the manpower acquired and the financial support obtained for the cause.

The proposed revolt of 1787 did not see the light of day because of an act of betrayal. Some priests and rebels betrayed the cause because of vested interests and fear of severe reprisals. This is the reality of human nature. But we should not persist with such a betrayal. We should not be traitors to one of Goa's pivotal and defining moments. It must be realized that the rebellion of 1787 in Goa impacted a similar one in Brazil, that occurred just two years later. Moreover while the American Revolution of 1776 was a revolution of British Americans and not of the natives of America, that in Goa, though aborted and unsuccessful, was purely nativistic.

APPENDIX 3.1

REBELS AND SUSPECTED REBELS ON TRIAL

Name	Profession / Post	Native Place	Residence	Age
Vincente de Abreu	Vargeiro	Chorão	Chorão	about 40
José Luis Guinete	Servant of Archbishop of Craganore	Milan, Italy	Santa Ines	about 25
Fr. Caetano da Silva	Vicar of S. Lourenço de Linhares	Sirula, Bardez	St. Lourenço de Linhares	not mentioned
Fr. Manoel da Expectação	Vicar of the Parish of Santa Anna, Ponda	Raya, Salcete	Ponda	41
Fr. João Alvares de Souza	Vicar of the Parish of Pomburpa	Pilerne	Pomburpa	58 (?)
Inacio Caetano Toscano	Tenente of the Legion of Bardez	Aldona	Aldona	32
Fr. Antonio Filipe Vas	Vicar of Moira	Piedade	Moira	49
Francisco Pereira	Ajundante de Cirurgia, Legion of Ponda	Carbolim	Carbolim	about 42

Fr. Miguel Alvares	Vicar of Pilerne	Pilerne	Pilerne	55
Nicolao Luis da Costa	Tenente of the Legion of Bardez	Parra	Parra	32
Fr. Caetano Francisco de Couto	Ecclesiastic; No post	Panjim	Panjim	45
Fr. Mathias Bernardo da Fonseca	Vicar of Chorão	Chorão	Chorão	43
Fr. Luis Antonio Gonsalves	Professor de Gramatica	Piedade	Piedade	32
Fr. Vicente Alvares	Ecclesiastic; No post	Pilerne	Pilerne	42
Baltazar Caeiro	Sargento of the Legion of Ponda	Assolna	Ponda	37
Manoel Ferrão	Cabo of the Legion of Ponda	Assolna	Ponda	30
Antonio Fernandes	Cabo of the Legion of Ponda	Verna	Ponda	about 40

Fr. Luis Caetano de Souza	Ecclesiastic; No post	Panjim	Panjim	about 52
Fr. José Manoel de Menezes	Vicar of Guirim	Piedade	Guirim	60
Fr. José Antonio Vas	Ecclesiastic; No post	Anjuna	Anjuna	about 32 (?)
Salvador Alvares da Costa	Was a Soldado	Parra	Parra	25
Fr. João Baptista Pinto	Ecclesiastic; No Post	Candolim	Candolim	about 32 (?)
João Vas	Soldado of the Legion of Ponda	Assolna	Ponda	40 (?)
Pedro Luis Gonzaga	Tenente of the Legion of Ponda	?	Ponda	?
Manoel Luis	Earned livelihood from farms	Candolim	Candolim	about 70
Manoel Caetano Pinto	Tenente of the Legion of Ponda	Candolim	Candolim	30 years
David Francisco Viegas	Cirurgião of the Legion of Ponda	Verem	Ponda	about 34

João de Souza Onorcar	Deportador de Cartas ou Recador; Businessman	Onor	Assolna	30
Sebastião de Noronha	Businessman	Nagoa, Salcete	Nagoa/Panjim	27-28
Fr. Sebastião Baptista	Clerigo Regular of Congregação do Oratorio	Verna	Convento de Santa Cruz de Milagres	about 44
Manoel Pinto	Livelihood from farms	Saligão	Saligão	30
José Monteiro	In Service	Taleigão	Taleigão	41
Bernardo de Mesquita	In Service	Penha de França	Penha de França	23-24
Inacio Caetano Lopes	Capitao dos Auxiliares, Legion of Ponda	Mandur	Mandur	32
Pascoal Lazaro	Distilled Wine	Santa Cruz	Santa Cruz	about 45
Fr. Diego Benedicto Lobo	Ecclesiastic; No post	Socorro	Socorro	45
Vitorino Vas	Vargeiro	Ilha de Capão	Ilha de Capão	about 31

Lourenço Fernandes	Vargeiro	Chorão	Chorão	30
Vicente Gomes	Vargeiro	Chorão	Chorão	about 46
Fr. Pedro Dalgado	Clergo Regular of the Congregação do Orotorio	Assagão	Convento de Santa Cruz dos Milagres	42
Filipe Fernandes	Begarim	Chorão	Chorão	about 42
Tomas Antonio Dias	Having own agency	Santa Ines	Santa Ines	about 30
Fr. Jorge Dias	Presbiteiro do Habito de São Pedro	Panjim	Panjim	32
Caetano Xavier da Costa	attached to Marechal	Chicalim	Ponda (?)	26-27
Miguel Antonio da Costa	Businessman	Chicalim	Panjim	30 (?)
Narba Naique	Cabo of one the Partidos; Sardessay	Ponda	Ponda	55

Source: AHU: *MI* Maço 155 (153), Devassa: *passim*.

APPENDIX 4.1

ASSEMBLIES / MEETINGS HELD BY REBELS

Sr. No.	Place / Location	Occasion/Date	No. of Days	Those Present/Involved
1.	Parochial House, Ribandar	Jan., 1787		Fr. José Antonio Gonsalves Fr. Pedro Dalgado
2.	Residence of the Pintos, Candolim	Before Lent/Entruso	2	Fr. José Antonio Gonsalves Fr. Caetano Francisco Couto Fr. João Baptista Pinto Manoel Caetano Pinto
		Around the Feast of São Pedro		Fr. José Antonio Gonsalves Fr. Caetano da Silva Fr. João Baptista Pinto José Luis Guinete
3.	Parochial House, Piedade	End of Jan./Beginning of Feb., 1787		Fr. José Antonio Gonsalves Fr. Pedro Dalgado

4.	Residence of Fr. José Antonio Gonsalves, Piedade	July, 1787		Fr. José Antonio Gonsalves Fr. Caetano da Silva Fr. Caetano Francisco de Couto Fr. Luis Antonio Gonsalves Sebastião de Noronha Pedro Luis Gonzaga
5.	Residence of Fr. Caetano Francisco Couto, Panjim	March, 1787		Fr. José Antonio Gonsalves Fr. Caetano Francisco de Couto
		Feast of Ascension, May, 1787		Fr. José Antonio Gonsalves Fr. Caetano Francisco de Couto Fr. Diego Caetano Couto Fr. Luis Caetano de Souza Salvador da Costa Fr. Inacio Monis
		Three days later in May, 1787		Fr. José Antonio Gonsalves Fr. Caetano Francisco de Couto Fr. Diego Couto Fr. Inacio Monis Sebastião de Noronha
		End of June, 1787		Fr. Caetano Francisco de Couto Fr. Diego Couto Caetano da Costa
		Before Feast of Santa Anna, July 26, 1787		Fr. Caetano Francisco de Couto Sebastião de Noronha

6.	Parochial House, Pilerne	Before Lent	Some days	Fr. José Antonio Gonsalves Fr. Caetano Francisco Couto Fr. João Bapitist Pinto Manoel Caetano Pinto Fr. Miguel Alvares
		After Lent	3	Fr. José Antonio Gonsalves Fr. Caetano Francisco Couto Fr. Miguel Alvares Manoel Francisco Gonsalves
		Beginning of June, 1787	5-6	Fr. José Antonio Gonsalves Fr. Miguel Alvares Fr. João Bapitist Pinto Luis Antonio Gonsalves José Luis Guinete
		Novenas, Respera and Feast of S. João, June 24, 1787	4-5	Fr. José Antonio Gonsalves Fr. Caetano Francisco Couto Fr. João Bapitist Pinto Fr. Caetano da Silva José Luis Guinete Fr. Miguel Alvares Fr. Vicente Alvares Fr. José Manoel Ribeiro Fr. José Caetano Rodrigues

		Beginning of July (?), 1787		Fr. José Antonio Gonsalves Fr. Caetano da Silva Manoel Caetano Pinto Fr. Miguel Alvares Inacio Toscano Fr. Diego Caetano de Couto Fr. José Manoel Ribeiro
		Novenas of Santa Anna, July 26, 1787	1	Fr. Miguel Alvares Fr. João Baptist Pinto Nicolau Luis da Costa Fr. José Antonio Gonsalves
		August 4,, 1787		Fr. Miguel Alvares Fr. José Antonio Gonsalves José Luis Guinete
7.	Residence of Fr. José Manoel Ribeiro, Pilerne	July, 1787		Fr. José Antonio Gonsalves Fr. Caetano da Silva Fr. José Manoel Ribeiro
		July, 1787		Fr. José Antonio Gonsalves Fr. José Vas Fr. José Manoel Ribeiro

8.	Residence of Fr. Vicente Alvares Pilerne	August 6, 1787	1	Fr. José Antonio Gonsalves Fr. Vicente Alvares Fr. José Manoel Ribeiro Geraldo Ferreira Rafael Marcos (?)
9.	Parochial House, Pomburpa	Around the Feast of Candeus, Feb. 2, 1787	4-5	Fr. José Antonio Gonsalves Fr. Caetano da Silva Fr. João Alvares de Souza José Luis Guinete Fr. Vicente Alvares Sebastião de Noronha
		Around Feb. 22, 1787	3-4	Fr. José Antonio Gonsalves Fr. João Alvares de Souza José Luis Guinete
		July 13 or 14, 1787	3	Fr. João Alvares de Souza Fr. José Antonio Gonsalves Fr. Diego Couto Sebastiao de Noronha
		Around the Feast of Santa Anna July 26, 1787	2-3	Fr. Gonsalves Fr. da Silva Fr. Joao Alvares Desouza Pedro Luis Gonzaga

10.	Residence of Manoel Pinto, Saligão	Feast of Santissma Trinidade, Beginning of June, 1787	2-3	Fr. José Antonio Gonsalves Fr. João Baptist Pinto Manoel Pinto José Luis Guinete
11.	Parochial House, Socorro	Around the Feast of S. Antonio, Beginning of June, 1787	7-8	Fr. José Antonio Gonsalves Fr. Caetano Francisco de Couto Fr. João Baptist Pinto Vicar of Socorro
12.	Parochial House, Moira	Around the Feast of N.S. do Carmo, July 16, 1787	4-5	Fr. José Antonio Gonsalves Fr. Caetano da Silva Nicolau da Costa Inacio Toscano
13.	Parochial House, Tivim	July 18, 1787	1	Fr. José Antonio Gonsalves Fr. Caetano da Silva Fr. Pedro Caetano José Lobo
14.	Parochial House, Anjuna	Beginning of July, 1787	Some days	Fr. José Antonio Gonsalves Fr. José Vas

15.	Residence of Avelino Francisco Lobo, Sirula	Mid -July	1-2	Fr. José Antonio Gonsalves Fr. Caetano da Silva Vicar of Church of Reys Magos Avelino Francisco Lobo
16.	Parochial House, Ponda	Feast of Santa Anna, July 26, 1787		Pedro Luis Gonzaga Sebastião de Noronha Fr. Manoel da Expectação

Source: AHU: *MI* Maço 155 (153), Devassa: *passim*

APPENDIX - 9.1

LIST OF THOSE ARRESTED BY DECEMBER 1787

Fr. Caetano Francisco de Couto.
Fr. Caetano da Silva, Vicar of S. Lourenço de Linhares.
Fr. João Baptista Pinto.
Tenente of the *Legião de Ponda*, Manoel Caetano Pinto.
Tenente of the same *Legião*, Pedro Luis Gonzaga.
Tenente of the *Legião de Bardez*, Nicolao Luis da Costa
Tenente of the same *Legião*, Inacio Caetano Toscano.
Vicente de Abreu
Italian José Luis Guinete
Fr. Manoel da Espectação, Vicar of Ponda.
Fr. João Alvares, Vicar of Pomburpa.
Fr. Antonio Filipe Vas, Vicar of Moira.
Francisco Pereira, Ajudante de Cirurgia of *Legião de Ponda.*
Fr. Miguel Alvares, Vicar of Pilerne.
Fr. Mathias Bernardo da Fonseca, Vicar of Chorão.
Fr. Luis Antonio Gonsalves.
Fr. Vicente Alvares.
Baltazar Caeiro Sargento of the *Legião de Ponda.*
Manoel Ferrão, Cabo of the said *Legião.*
Antonio Fernandes, Cabo of the same *Legião*
Fr. Luis Caetano de Souza.
Fr. José Manoel de Menezes, Vicar of Guirim
Fr. José Antonio Vas
Salvador da Costa.
João Vas, Soldado of *Legião de Ponda.*
Manoel Luis of Candolim.
David Francisco Viegas, Sargento of the *Legião de Ponda.*
João de Souza of Onor.
Sebastião de Noronha
Sebastião Baptista
Manoel Pinto of Saligão
José Monteiro.
Bernardo de Mesquita
Inacio Caetano Lopes, Capitão de Auxillares

Pascoal Lazaro
Fr. Diego Benedito Lobo
Vitorino Vas
Lourenço Fernandes
Vicente Gomes
Fr. Pedro Dalgado
Filipe Fernandes
Tomas Antonio Dias
Fr. Jorge Dias
Caetano Xavier da Costa
Miguel Antonio da Costa
Sardessay Narba Naique

LIST OF THOSE WHO FLED

Fr. José Antonio Gonsalves
Fr. José Manoel Ribeiro
Fr. Diego Caetano de Couto
Fr. Pedro Fernandes of Assagão

Source: AHU: *MI* doc.dtd. 15 Dec. 1787 signed by José Joaquim Sequeira Magalhaens e Lanções.

APPENDIX - 10.1

FRANCISCO DA CUNHA E MENEZES, GOVERNOR OF GOA (1786-1794)

APPENDIX - 11.1

ALFERES JOAQUIM JOSÉ DA SILVA (TIRADENTES)

APPENDIX - 11.2

MONUMENT OF TIRADENTES, PRAÇA TIRADENTES, OURO PRETO

BIBLIOGRAPHY

A. MANUSCRIPTS : ARCHIVAL SOURCES

1. Historical Archives of Goa

Monções do Reino

159B, 169A-169B, 170A-170C, 174B, 183, 186, 187A, 210A-210C

2. Arquivo Historico Ultramarino (Lisbon)

Maços de India

155(153)

C. PRINTED WORKS

Abreu, Miguel Vincente de, *O Governo do Vice-Rei Conde de Rio Pardo no Estado da India Portuguesa desde 1816 ate 1821*, Novo Goa, 1869

Avila, Cristina, "Ambiência Artística e Produção Iconográfica", *Cultura: Esdado de S. Paulo*, Ano VII, no. 456, 1989.

Azavedo, Carmo, "Pinto's Revolt of 1787", *Armed Coups Against Portuguese Regime*, Goa, 1986.

Barbuda, Claudio Lagrange Monteiro de, ed., *Instrucções que El Rei D. Joze mandou passar ao Estado da India no anno de 1774*, Nova Goa, 1841.

Boschi, Caio C, "O Bicentenário da Conjuração: O Que Comemorar?", *Cultura, Estado de S. Paulo*, Ano. VII, no. 456, 1989.

Boxer, C. R., *The Portuguese Seaborne Empire, 1415 - 1825*, The History of Human Society, gen.ed. J. H. Plumb, London, 1977.

Bruto da Costa, Roberto, *Hidra do Nativismo*, Nova Goa, 1920.

Carreira, Ernestina, "Goa in the Reign of Tipoo Sultan International Politics and the Pinto's Conspiracy", A paper presented at the Vth International Seminar on Indo-Portuguese History, Cochin, 1989.

Correia de Lima Almeida, Anita, "Goa de 1787 e Rio de Janeiro de 1794: Inconfidência no Imperio", *Portuguese Studies Review*, vol. IX, no. 112, 2001.

Cunha Rivara, Joaquim Heliodoro da, *A Conjuração de 1787 em Goa e varios cousas desse tempo*, Novo Goa 1875

____, *Goa and the Revolt of 1787*, ed. Charles J. Borges, transl. Renato da Cunha Soares, New Delhi, 1996.

Damante, Helio, "Tiradentes, Mito da Nacionalide", *Cultura: Estado de S. Paulo*, Ano VII, no. 456, 1989.

Dias, Mariano, "Fr. Caetano Vitorino de Faria", *Essays in Goan History*, ed. Teotonio R. de Souza, New Delhi, 1989.

Documentação Ultramarina Portuguesa, 5 vols., Centro de Estudos Historicos Ultramarinos, Lisboa, 1960-67.

Grieco, Donatello, *História Sincera da Inconfidência Mineira*, Rio de Janeiro, 1990.

Iglesias, Francisco, "O Clima Politico e a Articulação da Inconfidência", *Cultura: O Estado de S. Paulo*, Ano VII, no. 456, 1989.

Kamat, Pratima, *Farar Far. Local Resistance to Colonial Hegemony in Goa, 1510-1912*, Goa, 1999.

Martires Lopes, Maria de Jesus dos, "A Colónia Goesa em Lisboa e o Ideário da Conspiração dos Pintos (1787)", *Arquipélago*, Série Histórica, Ponta Delgada, vol. 1-1, 1995.

____, *Goa Setecentista. Tradição e Modernidade (1750-1800)*, Lisboa, 1996.

Maxwell, Kenneth R, *Conflicts and Conspiracies: Brazil and Portugal 1750-1808*, Cambridge University Press, 1973.

Mello e Souza, Laura de, "Os ricos, os probres nas Minas do seculo XVIII", *Cultura: O Estado de S. Paulo*, Ano VII, no. 456, 1989.

Moraes, G.M., "Contribution of Cunha Rivara to Indian Historiography", *India Past and Present*, 1, no.2, 1984.

____, "Padre Caetano Vitorino de Faria, a would be archbishop of Goa", *Boletim de Instituto Menezes Braganza*, no. 96, 1971.

Mota, Carlos Guilherme, "Do Discurso Sedicioso", *Cultura : O Estado de S. Paulo*, Ano VII, no. 456, 1989.

Pinto, Celsa, *Goa : Images and Perceptions. Studies in Goan History*, Goa, 1996.

____, *Trade and Finance in Portuguese India. A Study of the Portuguese Country Trade 1770-1840*, New Delhi, 1994.

Refutação Analytica d'Um Manifesto do Governo Intruzo de Goa, 1835.

Scarano, Julita, "Poema da Inconfidência", *Cultura: O Estado de S. Paulo*, Ano VII, no. 456, 1989.

Souza, Teotonio R. de, *Essays in Goan History*, ed., New Delhi, 1989.

____, *Indo-Portuguese History: Old Issues, New Questions*, New Delhi, 1985.

____, *Medieval Goa*, New Delhi, 1979

Subrahmanyam, Sanjay, *The Portuguese Empire in Asia, 1500-1700. A Political and Economic History*, London, 1993.

Xavier, Felippe Nery, *Collecção de Bandos e Outras Differentes Providencias Que Servem de Leis, Regulamentos Para O Governo Economico de Judicial Das Provincias Denominadas das Novas Conquistas*, 2 vols., Panjim, 1840-50.

Other publications from Broadway

Chaos
Vivek Nayak, Rs. 350/-, Pp.348, Pb., ISBN 9789380837413

A Woman's Guide to Sensible Eating
Rohini Diniz, Rs. 250/-, Pp.190, Pb., ISBN 9789380837420

Will Bombay be at Peace
Pradosh Karapurkar Rs. 195/- Pp.218 Pb. ISBN : 9789380837277

Rices of Goa & Their Grain Quality
Shilpa J. Bhonsle & S. Krishnan, Rs. 699/-, Pp. 155, Pb., ISBN 978819087912

Goa Rewound
Alexzndre Moniz Barbosa Rs. 195/- Pp.164 Pb. ISBN : 9789380837345

Being a Goan Christian
Victor Ferrao Rs. 195/- Pp.120 Pb. ISBN : 9789380837352

Goan Pioneers in Bombay
Teresa Albuquerque Rs. 295/- Pp. 227 Pb. ISBN : 9789380739236

Epistemology Search for Truth is made Easy
Antonio Rodrigues C.Ss.R. Rs. 150/- Pp. 186 Pb. ISBN: 9789380837369

Undra Muja Mama
Jose Pereira, Micael Martins & Antonio da Costa
Rs. 295/- . Pp. 210 Pb. ISBN : 9789380739267

Marine Fungi of India
B.D. Borse, D. J.Bhat, K. N. Borse, A.R. Tuwar, N. S. Pawar
Rs. 1995/- . Pp. 486 Hb. ISBN : 9789380837383

Choose Your Own Career
Basil D'Cunha, Rs.199/-, Pp. 293, Pb., ISBN 9789380837406

Infinite Articulation
Perin Ilavia Rs 495. Pp 81. Hb. ISBN 9789380837338

Goa Folklore studies
Dr. Pandurang Phaldesai. Rs 295. Pp 280. Pb. ISBN 9789380739229

Inhuman
Vivek Nayak. Rs 495. Pp 496. Pb. ISBN 9789380837284

Friendship Factor
Dr. U. G. Barad. Rs 395. Pp 368. Pb. ISBN 9789380837307

Take Control of Diabetes
Dr. U. G. Barad. Rs 295. Pp 265. Pb. ISBN 9789380837291

The Tulsi
Edila Gaitonde. Rs 195. Pp 160. Pb. ISBN 9789380739250

Goa Traffic
Marissa De Luna. Rs 350. Pp 260. Pb. ISBN 9789380837260

The Parish Churches of Goa: A Study of Façade Architecture
Jose Lourenço. Rs 595. Pp 220. Pb. ISBN 9789380837192

Konkani-Italiano Italian-Konknni dictionary
Ave Cleto Afonso. Rs 995. Pp 398. Hb. ISBN 9789380837215

Inside Out
Dr. U.G.Barad Rs 400. Pp 406. Pb ISBN 9789380837086.

Employment & Development in Goa
Silvia M. de Mendonça e Noronha Rs 395. Pp 125. Hb ISBN 9789380837093

English-Konkani Dictionary
Angelus F.X. Maffei Rs 695. Pp 545. Hb ISBN 9789380837161

Aroma
Shilpa Sinari. Rs 150. Pp 130. ISBN 9789380837079

Understanding Mahabharata
Raghupati Bhatt Rs 195. Pp 146. Pb ISBN 9789380837154.

Fascinating Microfungi (Hyphomycetes) of Western Ghats - India
Dr. Jayarama Bhat Rs. 1800. Pp 221.Pb ISBN 9789380837055.

Plant And Fungal Biodiversity &Bioprospecting
S. Krishnan Dr. D. J. Bhat Rs. 795. Pp 195. Pb ISBN 9789380837000.

The Cultural History of Goa
A. R. S. Dhume Rs 295. Pp 402. Hb ISBN 9788190571678.

Operation Vijay: The Ultimate Solution
Shrikant Y Ramani. Rs 495. Pp 402. Hb ISBN 9788190571661.

Information on the Right to Information
Anil A. Parulekar Rs. 250. Pb. ISBN 9788190571661

From Goa to Patagonia
Alfredo F. de Mello. Rs. 295. Pp. 215 ISBN 9788190571616 Hb.

Passionate and Unrestrained
Alexandre Barbosa (transl.) Rs. 225. Pb ISBN 9788190571647

Life is Beautiful
Tony Martin Rs 200. Pp 254. Pb. ISBN 9788190571623.

Mirror to Goa
Donna J. Young. Rs 195. Pp 169. Pb ISBN 9788190568210.

Practical English Teacher
Tony Martin. Rs. 125. Hb. ISBN 9788190571630

Into the Diaspora Wilderness
Selma Carvalho. Rs 345. Pp 270. ISBN 9789380739021

Modern Goan Literature: An anthology
Peter Nazareth (Ed.) Rs 395. Pp 420. Pb. ISBN 9788190568258.

The Sting of Peppercorns
Antonio Gomes. Rs 295. Pp 268. Pb. ISBN 978819056296.

Sur June Pan Noor Nava
Laxman Krishna Pitre. Rs. 99 Pp. 71 Hb. ISBN 9789380837031

Medieval Goa: A Socio-Economic History
Teotonio R. de Souza, Rs 495 (hb), Rs 395 (pb). Pp 265. ISBN 97881905682

Laxmanresha
Laxman Krishna Pitre. Rs. 180 Pp. 176 Hb. ISBN 9788190571623

Goa Masala
Rs.195 Pp.260 Pb. ISBN 9789380739045

The Cannons of Goa
Abhijit Ambekar, Rohini Pande and Tejas Garge. Rs. 795. Pp 80. Hb. ISBN 9789380837130

When the Curtains Rise
Andre Rafael Fernandes. Rs. 195 Pp. 215 Hb. ISBN 9789380739014

Patriotism in Action
Valmiki Faleiro Rs. 600 Hb. ISBN 9789380739069

Abbé Faria
Luis S. R. Vas Rs. 295 Hb ISBN 9788190571609

Inside Out : New Writing from Goa
Rs. 195 Pp. 244
ISBN 97893807391131

The Last Prabhu
Bernardo Elvino de Sousa
Rs.195 Pp. 163 ISBN 9789380739151

Francisco Luís Gomes 1829-1869
Luís De Assis Correa
Rs. 350 Pp., Rs 500 Hb 456

The Art of Coconut Craft
Vijaydatta Lotlikar
Rs. 195 Pp. 156. ISBN 9788190568234

Veni, Vidi... Goa
Luis S. R. Vas Rs 350. Pp 370. Hb. Rs. 295. Pp. 370 Pb.
ISBN 9789380837222

Glimpses From India's Natural World
A. K. Sahay. Rs 595. Pp 179. Pb. ISBN 9789380837123

Employment & Development in Goa
Silvia M. de Mendonça e Noronha Rs 395. Pp 125. Hb ISBN 9789380837093

English-Konkani Dictionary
Angelus F.X. Maffei Rs 695. Pp 545. Hb ISBN 9789380837161

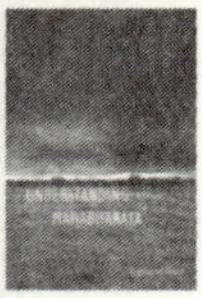

Aroma
Shilpa Sinari. Rs 150. Pp 130. ISBN 9789380837079

Understanding Mahabharata
Raghupati Bhatt Rs 195. Pp 146. Pb ISBN 9789380837154.

Fascinating Microfungi (Hyphomycetes) of Western Ghats - India
Dr. Jayarama Bhat Rs. 1800. Pp 221.Pb ISBN 9789380837055.

Plant And Fungal Biodiversity &Bioprospecting
S. Krishnan Dr. D. J. Bhat Rs. 795. Pp 195. Pb ISBN 9789380837000.

The Cultural History of Goa
A. R. S. Dhume Rs 295. Pp 402. Hb ISBN 9788190571678.

Operation Vijay: The Ultimate Solution
Shrikant Y Ramani. Rs 495. Pp 402. Hb ISBN 9788190571661.

Information on the Right to Information
Anil A. Parulekar Rs. 250. Pb. ISBN 9788190571661

From Goa to Patagonia
Alfredo F. de Mello. Rs. 295. Pp. 215 ISBN 9788190571616 Hb.

Passionate and Unrestrained
Alexandre Barbosa (transl.) Rs. 225. Pb ISBN 9788190571647

Life is Beautiful
Tony Martin Rs 200. Pp 254. Pb. ISBN 9788190571623.

Mirror to Goa
Donna J. Young. Rs 195. Pp 169. Pb ISBN 9788190568210.

Practical English Teacher
Tony Martin. Rs. 125. Hb. ISBN 9788190571630

Into the Diaspora Wilderness
Selma Carvalho. Rs 345. Pp 270. ISBN 9789380739021

Modern Goan Literature: An anthology
Peter Nazareth (Ed.) Rs 395. Pp 420. Pb. ISBN 9788190568258.

The Sting of Peppercorns
Antonio Gomes. Rs 295. Pp 268. Pb. ISBN 978819056296.

Sur June Pan Noor Nava
Laxman Krishna Pitre. Rs. 99 Pp. 71 Hb. ISBN 9789380837031

Laxmanresha
Laxman Krishna Pitre. Rs. 180 Pp. 176 Hb. ISBN 9788190571623

Medieval Goa: A Socio-Economic History
Teotonio R. de Souza, Rs 495 (hb), Rs 395 (pb). Pp 265.
ISBN 9788190568265.

UNDRA
MUJA
MAMA
Jose Pereira, Micael Martins
& Antonio da Costa

Epistemology
Search for Truth
is made easy

GOAN PIONEERS
IN BOMBAY
Teresa Albuquerque

BEING
A GOAN
CHRISTIAN
Victor Ferrao

GOA
REWOUND
Alexandre Moniz Barbosa

MARINEFUNGI
OF INDIA (MONOGRAPH)
B.D.Borse
D.J.Bhat
K.N.Borse
A.R.Tuwar
N.S.Pawar